"YOU OUGHT TO!"

"You Ought To!" is one of a series of low-cost books under the title PSYCHOANALYTIC **ideas** which brings together the best of Public Lectures and other writings given by analysts of the British Psychoanalytical Society on important psychoanalytic subjects.

The books can be ordered from:
Karnac Books
www.karnacbooks.com
Tel. +(0)20 7431 1075
Fax: +(0)20 7435 9076
E-mail: shop@karnacbooks.com

Other titles in the Psychoanalytic ideas Series:

Shame and Jealousy: The Hidden Turmoils
Phil Mollon

Dreaming and Thinking
Rosine Jozef Perelberg

Spilt Milk: Perinatal Loss and Breakdown
Joan Raphael-Leff (editor)

Unconscious Phantasy
Riccardo Steiner (editor)

Psychosis (Madness)
Paul Williams (editor)

Adolescence
Inge Wise (editor)

"YOU OUGHT TO!"

A Psychoanalytic Study of the Superego and Conscience

Bernard Barnett

Series Editors

Inge Wise and *Paul Williams*

Foreword by

Michael Parsons

KARNAC

First published in 2007 by the Institute of Psycho-Analysis, London

Karnac Books Ltd
118 Finchley Road
London
NW3 5HT

British Library Cataloguing in Publication Data

A C.I.P. for this book is available from the British Library

   ISBN 978 1 85575 983 1

Designed, typeset, and produced by The Studio Publishing Services Ltd
www.studiopublishingservicesuk.co.uk
e-mail: studio@publishingservicesuk.co.uk

Printed in Great Britain

10 9 8 7 6 5 4 3 2 1

www.karnacbooks.com

CONTENTS

CHAPTER SIX
The superego, the self, and morality: contemporary

*With gratitude for their love to all members of my present family
and to those no longer with us and who are of blessed memory*

ACKNOWLEDGEMENTS

This book has been composed and produced, in a very part-time manner, over a period of approximately eight years. During this period my family and many colleagues and friends have greatly helped in its conception, production, and completion, and I wish to thank them all for their support and encouragement.

I begin with Dr Jennifer Johns who, in 1995, was chair of the committee responsible for the introductory public lectures held at the Institute of Psychoanalysis. She invited me to give an annual lecture on the superego for three consecutive years, and the preparation for this event led to the accumulation of the material which stimulated the writing of the book.

I wish to give special thanks to the members of my family for their tolerance and for the time that I spent away from them researching the superego and tapping away on the word processor. I am especially grateful to my wife, Ruth, for her love, which sustained me, and for her time spent in reading, commenting on, and discussing the many earlier drafts of the chapters. I also want to thank my son, Bruce, for his careful proof reading, and for correcting my writing, spelling, and grammar, and for his valiant (but largely failed) attempt to teach me the craft of using commas appropriately. I also thank my daughter, Tania, and my son, Barry, for their encouragement in my work and for our many discussions on literary texts. Thanks, too, to my son-in-law, Tom, for his help with proofs, and with the bibliography, proof reading and, on occasion, with my computer problems.

Of the numerous colleagues and friends with whom I have discussed the book over its long period of gestation, I wish to thank Donald Campbell and Michael Parsons for their early encouragement and their thoughtful comments.

With regard to my initial training in English literature, I wish to acknowledge the contribution of Professor Frank Kermode, who stimulated in me a love of English literature. For our ongoing discussions on the relationship between the superego and literature and for enriching my thinking about William Shakespeare, George Eliot, and James Joyce, I thank my friends Joan Byles, Beatrice Clarke, and Gerald Normie.

With regard to my psychoanalytic training, knowledge, and experience, I wish to acknowledge the huge debt that I owe to Pearl King for the application of her skill and her quiet patience with me over many years, and the late Tom Haley for his skilled help and support. To both, I am grateful for their marvellous (if sometimes painful) creative excursions with me into the unconscious.

I especially thank all my child, adolescent, and adult patients, whom I have seen in London and who have shared with me their inner lives, playfulness, and wisdom.

For her supervision of my work, I wish to acknowledge my gratitude to Edna O'Shaughnessy. Also, for their expert psychoanalytic teaching and supervision, I give thanks to Paula Heimann, John Klauber, Adam Limentani, Harold Stewart, Marion Milner, Enid Balint, John Padell, Nina Coltart, Sidney Klein, and Martha Harris, who are, sadly, no longer with us.

For many stimulating discussions, I wish to thank my friends and colleagues, Sharon Stekelman, David Riley, John Keene, Ken Robinson, Marianne Parsons, Felicity Dirmeik, Judith Szekacs, Brian Jacobs, Bernice Krickler, Siobhan O'Connor, Kami Ghaffari, Leon Kleimberg, Harold Blum, and Sidney Blatt, among many others.

I have also learnt a great deal that is relevant to the themes of this book from those psychoanalytic colleagues and students in London, Newcastle, and Northern Ireland, who have attended my theoretical and clinical seminars over many years.

I offer my thanks to Jim McLean and my friend, Michael Schachter, for their computer expertise and technical help, and to Clemmie Jacques and the Institute library staff for their assistance with the bibliography. I am also very grateful to Karen, Teresa, and the Tavistock Library staff for help over many years.

Last, but not least, a special thank you is due to my general editors, Paul Williams and Inge Wise, for their sustained encouragement and confidence that I would one day get the job done in spite of my own doubts, deliberations, and delays.

Quotations from *Consciousness and the Novel: Connected Essays* by David Lodge, published by Secker & Warburg, are reprinted by permission of the Random House Group Ltd.

Bernard Barnett
March 2007

ABOUT THE AUTHOR

Bernard Barnett is a fellow of, and Training analysist in, the Institute of Psychoanalysis. He is qualified in child analysis and has taught at the Institute for many years. He was formerly Chair of the Education Committee.

He previously held the post of Director of Psychological Training at the Child Guidance Training Centre and at the Tavistock Centre in the Department of Children and Families.

He has a special interest in Independent Psychoanalytic Thinking and Holocaust Studies. He is currently Director of the Squiggle Foundation. He works in private practice in London and is married with three children and two grandchildren.

FOREWORD

The superego is one of those psychoanalytic concepts that has been assimilated into ordinary language, like repression, the unconscious, and the Oedipus complex. Because it has become such a familiar notion, its complexity may not always be appreciated, nor the controversy that it can inspire. Its origins, for example, its timing in the course of development, whether and how it is influenced by gender—all these questions and others have been the source of lively disagreement. For psychoanalysts, it is a fundamental concept of their discipline, but it belongs to a meta-psychology whose value is often questioned, and opinions might vary on whether it remains truly alive as a generative, energizing idea in contemporary psychoanalysis.

A compact but comprehensive survey, therefore, of the concept of the superego is very much to be welcomed. Bernard Barnett, a training analyst of the British Psychoanalytic Society, has for a long time been appreciated as a teacher there. His thoroughness and his systematic approach are evident in this book. Starting with an account of how Freud elaborated, over many years, the idea of an agency within a person's mind that monitors and passes judgement on the person, Barnett goes on to describe the evolution of the superego from infancy to adulthood. He considers different views of this development and its chronology, and also how various analytic orientations have conceptualized the operation of the mature superego. With an examination of the Holocaust, he shows how the superego's functioning can go catastrophically wrong. He concludes by reflecting on what relation the concept of the superego may have to postmodern ideas about the decentred self.

George Eliot's novel *Daniel Deronda* runs like a thread through the book. In almost every chapter, Barnett draws on it for illustrations. If one knows the novel, this book reads like a psychological running commentary on it. For readers who do not know *Daniel Deronda*, it will probably be the next book picked up after this one. In fact, this book will send its readers to a variety of others. A compact survey does not aim to go into every topic in depth, and Barnett has done an admirable job, particularly with his notes, in signposting readers where to look next and encouraging them to do so.

This is a book to be taken as a whole. More than once I found myself thinking as I was reading, "But Bernard, you can't just say that and leave it there!" And of course he does not. Later in the chapter, or in the next one, the train of thought picks up what may seem to have been left in a siding. For all its small size, Bernard Barnett's book makes some demands on the reader, and so much the better. No one will finish it without both being informed and having their own thinking stimulated.

Michael Parsons

"It was a dreadful thing to see. Human beings *can* be awful cruel to one another . . . so we poked along back home, and I warn't feeling so brash as I was before, but kind of ornery, and humble, and to blame, somehow—though I ain't done nothing. But that's always the way; it don't make no difference whether you do right or wrong, a person's conscience ain't got no sense and just goes for him *anyway*. If I had a yaller dog that didn't know no more than a person's conscience does I would pison him"

(Mark Twain, *Huckleberry Finn*, 1884, original italics)

". . . Ah he thought, the truth bursting on him suddenly, nobody grows up. Everyone carries around all the selves that they have ever been, intact, waiting to be reactivated in moments of pain, of fear, of danger. Everything is retrievable, every shock, every hurt . . ."

(Anita Brookner, *Latecomers*, 1988, p. 210)

CHAPTER ONE

Introduction

"Were uneasiness of conscience measured by extent of crime, human history had been different and one should look to see the contrivers of greedy wars and the mighty marauders of the money-market in one troop of self-lacerating penitents with the meaner robber and cut-purse and the murderer that doth his butchery in small with his own hand. No doubt wickedness hath its rewards to distribute; but whoso wins in this devil's game must need be baser, more cruel, more brutal than the order of this planet will allow for the multitude born of women, the most of these carrying a form of conscience—a fear which is the shadow of justice, a pity which is the shadow of love—that hindereth from the prize of serene wickedness, itself difficult of maintenance in our composite flesh"

(Eliot, 1876)

"Born dependent, impulse ridden, fickle, egoistic, body bound, we grow up—if the Fates do but grant us grace—into independent, controlled (but spontaneous), constant, reasonably unselfish, spiritually far seeing and yet body-enjoying adults . . .

1

One of the means by which this remarkable transformation
takes place is through the process of superego formation"

(Rickman, 1950)

I n this book I seek a greater understanding of that which George
Eliot refers to as "the devil's game". That is, I attempt a description, clarification, and exploration of certain conscious ideas
and more deeply rooted unconscious ones that interact and relate
to the growth and presence of "good" and "bad", "right" and
"wrong", and morality and immorality, in the human psyche.
Although my main focus is on the modern Freudian and post-
Freudian theoretical exploration of the superego, the ego ideal, and
so-called "unconscious guilt", I also discuss the more traditional
and more familiar ideas such as conscience, conscious guilt, and
remorse and their relationship to psychoanalytic theory.

This chapter is concerned with a description of the main features
of what I shall refer to as *the system superego*.[1]

These are clarified and illustrated by means of simple case
vignettes taken from clinical practice, press reports, and English
literature.

The book is concerned with the nature of the superego system,
its normal and abnormal development in the individual person,
and some implications of how the system functions in relation to
society as a whole.

I begin with a few examples that seek to illustrate the pathological or mal-development of the system at various levels of complexity.

Oxford undergraduate

A daily newspaper described the case of a young Oxford undergraduate, the president of the union, who had recently been
expelled from the university for cheating. The reporter had
commented on certain features of her personality and background.
For example, that she had set herself very high standards and had
acted under "pressure" of trying to combine student politics with
her final examination. It was also said that she was "driven" by the
achievement of an older sister, who had obtained first class honours

at the same university. The journalist also reported that the young woman had attended a public school and that the school had a stated aim "to teach girls to govern themselves and their conduct by their reason and conscience". When asked to comment on the incident, the headmistress had suggested that the cheating behaviour had been "out of character" and that the student had been one of "the best brains I have taught".[2]

Laboratory technician

A newspaper reported on the case of a fifty-seven-year-old laboratory technician who, posing as a doctor, had committed indecent assaults on women for his own sexual and other gratification. He was described as having carried out worthless cervical smears and HIV tests for profit, and had thus misled female patients, leaving them in a dangerous situation, exposed and at risk. He had also managed to pose as an expert witness on behalf of accused drink drivers, for which he charged £8,000 a time. This man was found guilty of assault, wounding, and obtaining money by deception. He was described by the judge as a "one man medical crime wave" and was jailed for five years. In a reference he had previously written on his own behalf, he had said, "Onubogu is an enigma who we all admire and glorify".[3]

A "hit and run" incident

A policeman was engaged in waving down a speeding driver. When he attempted to stop the car, he was hit and dragged for fifty yards along the road and fatally injured. The car, which then failed to stop, was later found abandoned and subsequently two men and a woman were arrested.[4]

A patient's envious/jealous superego

K was a patient being treated in a psychiatric hospital. The analyst in charge of his case reported the following material: K had formed a relationship with H, a female patient, and they had successfully

made love. However, immediately after love-making, K had stran-
gled H and then presented himself to the police and confessed
to murder. He was tried before a court, but pleaded that the cou-
ple had been playing sex games at H's request. This plea was
accepted by the court and he was given a short sentence (Sohn,
2000).

Discussion

These four examples have been selected to illustrate the range of
behaviour that can be associated with ideas of conscience, guilt, and
the pathological superego. In each case, the part of the mind linked
to these ideas is seen to function in an abnormal or highly unusual
way. In each, the individual concerned was, to a different degree,
side-stepping the commonly experienced inner restraints on
"uncivilized" behaviour.

Each example represents a different aspect of "the devil's game"
and each provides, to a lesser or greater degree, an illustration of
the malfunctioning of the system superego. A measure of the failure involved is shown by the degree to which (in George Eliot's
words) "fear" and "pity", "justice" and "love", have made way for
the prize of "serene wickedness".

The example of the Oxford undergraduate appears to illustrate
an isolated breakdown of conscience under certain specific environmental conditions. It seems that specific external and internal
"pressures" (i.e., finals examination and the envy of a sister) had
resulted in an impulsive, "atypical", unethical act in a vulnerable
personality. In this case, the comments of the student's former
headmistress also illustrates something of her own ideals of "self-
government" and of educating and handing on to the university
"the best brains". What is clear is that this young student had failed
to live up to the standards that had been laid down for her. The case
also provides an illustration of the *internalized other*, a representation of parental (and other influential) standards and values
present in the mind and the gap between it and conscience, or
rather, a failure of conscience. An elaboration of the complicated
processes that are associated with this discrepancy are further
described and illustrated in Chapters Two and Three.

The case of the laboratory technician clearly demonstrates a very much more serious situation from the social point of view. This man's crimes point to an extreme and prolonged failure of superego constraints at a psychopathic level. The well-planned and premeditated criminal acts, which were closely linked to sexual, aggressive, and financial gratification, had resulted in extremely harmful consequences for other people. In this instance, even on this limited evidence, the man's criminal and sadistic behaviour can also be linked to certain features of his personality, in which extreme omnipotence, pathological narcissism, and naked greed appear to combine with a total absence of identification and empathy with the victims.

In the third example, which involved a hit and run incident, the environmental situation involved a group of persons acting together in a very seriously delinquent way. The incident reported appears to illustrate a mixture of so-called "road rage" with what may have been a panic reaction. This lethal combination appears to have produced an impulsive and murderous act when the victim was seen as interfering with the criminal behaviour. In this instance, the norms of civilized conduct were apparently over-ridden, and this resulted in the death of a mildly threatening (although perhaps not seen as such), anonymous authority figure. This example provides another instance of the complete lack of empathic identification with another human being, one that resulted in the victim's loss of life.

My final illustration is taken from the psychiatric patient population to illustrate a particular type of superego pathology. It has been chosen to show how the grossly abnormal functioning of the superego can lead to an attack and weakening of the ego-self, which has abdicated control of the personality. The end result of this process leads in this instance to behaviour that is both self-harming and other-destructive.

The psychoanalyst who reports the case describes the pathological process along the following lines. The schizophrenic patient K came from an extremely disturbed background that was associated with delinquent parents, care orders, residential schools, drug taking (and "pushing"), and abandonment. The patient had idealized his absent mother and felt himself to be responsible for her delinquent actions. In communicating his understanding of the clinical material, the analyst (working in the Kleinian tradition) suggested to the patient that his act of making love to another patient, H, had been related to a psychotically envious part of K's mind. The analyst's conclusion was that "the envious superego" had madly and jealously overviewed K's relationship to H, and had attacked it, and that this had resulted in the murder of H. In court, K's presentation of H as sexually abnormal was, according to the analyst, an attempt to appease his own envious/jealous superego. A number of different theoretical approaches to the superego's attack on the self, and on the other, will be found in Chapters Four and Five.

In the examples illustrated above, there is evidence that something had gone wrong with the operation of the usual restraints on behaviour that accompany a "normally functioning" superego, conscience, and sense of guilt. The rest of the book is concerned with the further, detailed exploration of the individual features of this superego system, in healthy development and in abnormal behaviour.

A selection of explanatory concepts[5]

In the illustrations and discussion above, the term *superego* and other related concepts have been used loosely and without further explanation or definition. In what follows, some attempt will be made to clarify them, at least in so far as they are used by the present writer. It should, nevertheless, be borne in mind that there is much overlap in meaning in these concepts, and that most of the differences described below are mainly matters of preference and emphasis, rather than substance.[6]

The "system superego"

In its broadest terms, this system covers aspects of the mind that are directly and indirectly associated with internal and external morality. The system is an umbrella term for a number of closely related concepts: superego (narrow meaning), ego ideal, the ego, the self, the conscience, the sense of guilt, the wish for punishment and remorse. In the widest sense, the functions of the system include observation of the ego, the setting of values and standards, making judgements, and inflicting self (and other) punishments. This process consists of a complex interplay of elements, involving conscious and unconscious aspects of the various functions, and these are discussed below.

The superego (narrow meaning)[7]

In its most limited sense, the term superego can be understood to refer to that part of a person's mind that watches over the ego, judges it, criticizes it, and punishes it. It is mainly unconscious and derives its energy from deeply unconscious sources (i.e., from "the id"). As exemplified in the case illustrations above, this part of the mind can act upon *the ego-self* and/or *the other* sternly, cruelly, and murderously, but it can also adopt a more benign and loving attitude.[8]

The ego ideal

The ego ideal and the superego are closely related and not easily distinguishable. In the overall system, the superego "hovers" over the ego–self, keeps it under observation and judges its thoughts and actions. The ego ideal thus overlaps with this superego function of the mind, but it also offers the ego possibilities towards which it can aim. It is in this sense that the ego ideal can be understood as a representation of *the standards* by means of which the superego judges the ego and determines the way in which the subject must behave in order to respond to the superego's authority.[9]

Since this ideal was first developed by the subject's internalization of qualities derived from the primary caring figures in early childhood, it also has conscious and unconscious aspects. It stands apart from *the ego-self*, partly on account of its idealized character. It inherits the early mental state of narcissistic perfection, a developmental stage when the subject is merged in a perfect, gratifying union with the caring figure. It also plays a crucial role in ongoing mental development, since the subject seeks to repossess and restore the original omnipotence and the lost perfection of the narcissistic stage by projecting the ego ideal into the mother, who is the first ego ideal. This restorative aim gives rise to the fantasy of reunion with the mother (when, for example, a metaphorical "Garden of Eden" will be re-established). Since such perfection cannot be achieved in reality, the ego ideal only offers the subject an illusionary "approximation" to fulfilment. It is, therefore, always to be experienced as a journey without arrival. The role and function of the ego ideal is fantasy based on the mother–child relationship. In this sense, the ego ideal contrasts with the superego, in that the latter acts to strengthen reality and to increase the psychic distance between the subject and the mothering figure (Chasseguet-Smirgel, 1975).

The ego-self's relationship to the ego ideal consists of a desire to improve in accordance with its standards. In contrast, its relationship to the superego is more closely linked to feelings of anxiety caused by failed aspirations. The tendency is for the idealizing and criticizing aspects of the system to work in opposition rather than co-operatively, and this may result in both common and pathological experiences of self-hatred (Blos, 1972).

Conscience

A person's conscience is typically described as an "inner voice" and, in that sense, it is close to conscious awareness and human consciousness in general.[10]

The conscience is clearly a very old and much described idea, and can perhaps be dated back to the notion of Adam and Eve's exclusion from the Garden of Eden. It has been frequently observed that conscience (which may be simply defined as the "consciousness" of the effect of one's actions) though a highly valued human attribute, can also be seen as a curse in so far as it may be associated with a tragic dimension of living. As the vignettes above seek to illustrate, to be human is to be capable of doing almost anything "bad" (or "good").

As I have already mentioned, there is a large and comprehensive literature on the concept of conscience that has stimulated the members of many disciplines to write about it. Such contributions have come from theologians, philosophers, psychologists, anthropologists, and writers of literature, as well as from psychoanalysts.

The following description of conscience has been provided by a psychoanalyst writing in 1945. Its value lies in the clarity of the distinction that he draws between "conscience" and "instinct" in mental functioning, and in its stress on individual differences:

> A superimposed factor of acquired direction and control, a factor which is in some sense less "natural" and "spontaneous" than instinct, and which bids its possessor now to proceed more vigorously in some direction than his instincts would dictate, now to desist from some action which to his instincts would appear desirable . . . this controlling moral agency operates over a wide field of human activities and tends to function more regularly and consistently in some individuals than others . . . [Flugel, 1945, pp. 17, 23]

Another valuable approach to the investigation of conscience can be found in literary sources, and especially in a number of Shakespeare's plays. For example, in his recent introduction to *Macbeth*, an eminent critic writes as follows:

> . . . Macbeth is an Everyman: and for him . . . the guilt that is at first a matter of choice, becomes, as his will atrophies, a matter of fate. His torments of conscience no longer come between desire and act. He loses his distinctive humanity. . . . He knows the terrors of conscience and imagines an appalling future after the crime "nothing is/but what is not" . . . his wife loses her mind in guilt . . . [this is] the greatest of the plays about human guilt . . . [that is] a fierce engagement between the mind and its guilt. [Kermode, 1997, pp. 1357–1358] (See also Lukacher, 1994.)

The ego and the self

In the discussion so far, the terms *ego* and *self* have been more or less used interchangeably. In examining the system superego, I shall first try to distinguish them. However, in the psychoanalytic usage of the two terms, there is a considerable overlap. Therefore, as a matter of convenience, in much of the discussion that follows I use them as a single (hyphenated) concept.[11]

The self can be thought of as closer to the more personal and direct conscious experience, and the ego to the more impersonal and unconscious. Because, strictly speaking, the psychic structures (i.e., id, ego, superego) are never directly experienced (though they are responsible for generating experience), they can never be *personal* in the sense implied in the word "self".

The ego refers to an organized, structured part of the mind that has its origins in the id (i.e., the unorganized, undifferentiated, instinctual part of the mind and the seat of the passions) and which is that part modified by the external world. The ego also represents reason and common sense and it borrows its energy from the id. It is also a product of internalizing the other (typically, though not exclusively, one's early experience of a mother and a father).

The ego and the self also differ in relation to their frames of reference. The former is understood as a structure which belongs to the objective frame of reference and its functions can be described in terms of impersonal generalizations. In contrast, the self (or strictly speaking "a sense of self") is a phenomenological concept closely connected with the essence of consciousness. It, therefore, belongs to a subjective frame of reference and to the notion of personal experience (see Rycroft, 1968, pp. 149–150).

Remorse and "the sense of guilt"

In the system superego, the idea of *remorse* is closely associated with *the sense of guilt* and it is again convenient to consider them together. In everyday usage, remorse has been defined as deep regret and repentance for a wrong committed and also as compassionate reluctance to inflict pain on others, as in the phrase "without remorse", in which its absence is emphasized (Brown, 1993; Church, 1991, p. 214).

Psychoanalytic theory is more or less in agreement with this description in that a sense of guilt may be experienced by the subject after a misdeed has actually been committed (Freud, 1930a, p. 131).

The experience of guilt also presupposes the development of a system superego. However, the superego theory also includes an important extension to this definition in its recognition of the significance of guilty states of mind which are unconscious and which do *not* relate to *actual* crimes and misdeeds carried out by the subject. That is, from the superego standpoint, for the subject to experience guilt, it is sufficient that something "wrong" is *felt* to have occured.

The total absence of genuine remorse in the subject after a crime has been committed (e.g., the case of the fake doctor above), suggests an extreme malfunctioning of the superego system and one which, for example, can be very influential in verdicts and sentences in courts of law.

The sense of guilt has significant conscious (related to conscience and awareness) and unconscious (related to the superego) features and these are further considered throughout the book.

Need for punishment

A very close ally of the sense of guilt and remorse, is the *need for self-punishment*, although it is helpful in comparing normality and pathology to consider this concept separately. Instances of self-punishment have been found in psychoanalytic dream research and, from the abnormal standpoint, observations of a tendency to self-punishment are especially prominent in research into obsessional neurosis and melancholia (see Chapter Two).

In obsessional neurosis, the phenomena appear as patterns of self-reproach and punitive forms of behaviour in that the patient's symptoms are a torment to him. In melancholia, the compulsion to self-punishment may ultimately lead to the patient's suicide, although unconsciously this action is also understood psychoanalytically as "*other*-punishment". The discovery of the "negative therapeutic reaction" has also pointed to the patient's tendency and determined need to punish himself by holding on to his illness and suffering, in the face of the analyst's best efforts to help him.

Such self-punishing attitudes and behaviour can also be understood as produced by a tension between a particularly demanding, critical, and punitive superego and a passive and submissive ego. However, following Freud, some analysts find the origin of a need for self-punishment in a death instinct, a "force tending towards the destruction of the subject" and one which is fundamental to the

human situation and not reducible to a tension between the sub-
systems of the mind as described in this section.[12]

Morality

The last concept to be considered in this chapter is that of morality,
which, from the analytic point of view, is closely connected with the
system superego. It should be clear from the discussion so far that,
according to psychoanalytic theory, the creation of this system has a
special role in the individual personality, in so far as it is the *agent of
morality*. The superego system has this role because of its connection
with primary others in the individual's past life, and because of its
current interaction with the ego-self (including the awareness of
one's own subjectivity) and with the instinctual impulses/id (i.e.,
"an assortment of desires and drives directed towards their objects").

However, the id does not constitute a separate self, but only
becomes part of the self-system when taken up by consciousness (i.e.,
when its influence becomes, in some sense, acknowledged by the
subject). Although a superego system in the personality is essential
to the growth of morality and to the maintenance of civilization, its
malfunctioning may also have significantly harmful effects (see the
case studies above that illustrate "rebellious delinquency" and
"pathological murderousness"), and these may, of course, be detrimental to the individual and to society. These negative effects may,
at least to some extent, be reduced by the strengthening and expan-
sion of the ego-self in its struggle with the unrealistic and oppressive
aspects of the superego system.

The similarity of the four concepts, guilt, remorse, punishment,
and morality, can be seen to be close in the instance when we are
"commanded" by the superego. Morality involves a sense of duty
reflected in the "ought" aspect of living in relation to one's self and
one's culture. The superego system is thus closely associated with the
predominant morality of the society in which the individual lives.
Thus, although the internalization process in the subject begins with
the primary carers, it gradually accumulates into an amalgam of
different individual influences. It is in this way that the system
increasingly becomes an abstract representation of a particular
society.

Examples and illustrations from Daniel Deronda[13]

In the following chapters, I will illustrate my discussion of different aspects of the superego system described above by drawing freely on the work of nineteenth century writer, George Eliot, whose expressed aim was "to widen the English vision a little . . . and let in a little conscience and refinement".

Her last novel, *Daniel Deronda*, was published in 1876, and is particularly relevant to my theme, since it offers a "pre-Freudian" exploration of what the author calls "the unmapped country within us which would have to be taken into account in an explanation of our gusts and storms . . . the hidden pathways of feeling and thought which lead up to every moment of action" (see note 13, pp. 157, 265).

To enable the reader unacquainted with this novel to follow the illustrations that are used in the present work, a brief synopsis of the plot is given below.

Daniel Deronda is a fictional account of the growth of self in a young man, and the growth of conscience in a young woman. The growth of self concerns the character, Daniel, who is in his twenties and is a person who has grown up without knowledge of his biological mother or father. He has been reared and educated by a rich, upper-class and kindly guardian ("uncle"), Sir Hugh Malinger, whose aim has been to make him into an English gentleman. Unaware of his actual roots, he harbours the fantasy that he is the uncle's illegitimate son. Eliot's portrayal is of a "lost" person, in search of an identity and a vocation that would give meaning to his "rootless" existence. Portrayed as a "selfless" person, he has an idealistic frame of mind, which leads to "an extension of sympathy" towards others and to altruistic acts of rescue.

The development of conscience is illustrated in the heroine, Gwendolen Harleth, who is aged twenty-one. She is portrayed as beautiful, clever, high-spirited, and socially confident, but also as a "spoiled child". In contrast to Daniel, she is egoistic and self-absorbed, is very close to her mother, and also occasionally exhibits "hysterical" outbursts. She appears as "cold" and she complains that she cannot love anyone. However, she meets and is impressed by an aristocratic man, aptly named Mr Grandcourt.

1. 10

1. 55

Henleigh Malinger Grandcourt is thirty-six and the nephew of Daniel's guardian. He has an inscrutable manner and strangely inert reserve, and these impress Gwendolen as "calm, cold manners". She fantasizes that he will be "manageable" as a husband. In fact, he is ruled by an excess of egotism and, though attracted to and challenged by Gwendolen, his real intent is to marry in order to tame and control her. However, his former mistress, Lydia Glasher, by whom he has four children, confronts Gwendolen and tells her that Grandcourt ought to marry her, Lydia. On gaining this information, Gwendolen rejects Grandcourt and runs away to the continent.

Another major character is Gwendolen's mother, Mrs Davilow. She is portrayed as a timid and depressed woman (one who demonstrates "habitual melancholy") who is dominated by Gwendolen. We learn that Gwendolen's father had died when she was very young, and that the mother had remarried and produced four half-sisters, whom Gwendolen jealously resents. We also learn that, at the time of the action, her step-father is dead.

The action of the novel begins, as it were, *in medias res*, when Daniel is observing and being observed by Gwendolen, whom he sees gambling in a casino. She begins to lose and has subsequently to pawn a necklace. He recovers the necklace and returns it to her anonymously. She reacts to this gesture with anger and humiliation, but, at another level, senses his interest in and empathy towards her.

When Gwendolen learns that her family are threatened by poverty, she agrees to marry Grandcourt. However, on her wedding night, after reading a threatening letter from Lydia Glasher, she bursts into hysterical screams. This is an omen for an unhappy marriage and Gwendolen shares her sadness about this with Daniel, who has become a kind of father-confesser and counsellor and is gradually being internalized as part of her conscience.

Daniel encounters a beautiful eighteen-year-old Jewish woman called Mirah, who has escaped from an abusive father and has attempted suicide. Daniel, however, rescues her and places her with a supportive family. Gradually, he becomes attracted to Mirah and interested in her Judaism. This leads him to meet a Jewish family and a scholarly Jew called Mordecai, who is consumptive and terminally ill. Mordecai is also searching for a healthy soul-mate in whom to implant his dream of going to a Jewish homeland. He makes a strong impression on Daniel, who also discovers that he (Mordecai) is, in fact, Mirah's lost brother, and, in another act of altruism, he reunites the two.

Daniel learns that his mother, a Jewess and a singer of international reputation, is alive and wishes to meet him. Now, at last, he is told by his guardian, Sir Hugo, that his father is dead. He meets his mother, who tells him of her family history, his Jewish roots and of his birth, rejection, and adoption by Sir Hugo. She also tells him that she is "not a loving woman" and that she is terminally ill. However, given this information about his background, Daniel now feels free to court and marry Mirah.

Gwendolen is increasingly unhappy and oppressed in her marriage, which is ended when Grandcourt is drowned in a boating accident. However, she is left with painful guilt feelings arising from her death wishes towards her husband and from her hesitant behaviour in making a rescue attempt. She talks to Daniel about these feelings, and he supports and comforts her.

The novel ends with Daniel's marriage to Mirah and their decision to emigrate to Palestine. When Gwendolen is told of these plans, although she feels utterly forsaken by Daniel, she reacts to her profound loss with strength and dignity. In an acknowledgement of the internalization, she says, "It is better—it shall be better with me because I have known you".

In my description of the various aspects of the growth and characteristics of a superego system in the following chapters, I shall continue to use the characters and plot of the novel as illustration (see also Wilson, 1984).

Notes

1. The word "system" is adopted here because the various concepts mentioned above "hang together" and interact in a complex manner.
2. *The Times*, 10 September, 1998.
3. *The Independent*, 9 September, 1998.
4. *The Independent*, 20 December, 2000.
5. The main aspects of the "system" and their application that are described in this book are clearly not an exhaustive account of the concepts and various interactions. See for example, the chapter headings in Flugel (1945) for a comprehensive coverage in the context of a wider society.

6. Freud himself, though aware of his loose use of terms, was, nevertheless, somewhat reluctant to refine his complex system, perhaps because he wished to emphasize the significance of the overlap of the concepts. For example, see Freud, (1933a, p. 136).

7. I shall attempt throughout to use the term "superego" to cover only the narrower definition, though it is a difficult task to be entirely consistent in this usage and I am aware of not always succeeding.

8. In *The Ego and the Id* (Freud, 1923b), the loving aspect of the superego is noted but not developed, but see in this respect Fenichel (1945), Schafer (1960), Milrod (1972), and Sandler (1987).

9. For a different definition, see Flugel (1945).

10. "Another's voice . . . need not be experienced as spatially external to me . . . it is enough that it addresses itself to me . . . the voice of another may influence me as I merely deliberate about what to do; it will influence mere intentions to act" (Church, 1991, p. 216).

11. It is important to note that, in his use of the concept of *Das Ich*, Freud does not distinguish between the impersonal ego and the personal "I" but rather, in his theorizing, shifts from one domain to the other (Modell, 1993).

12. For a full discussion of self-punishment, see Laplanche and Pontalis (1973, pp. 260–261).

13. The edition of *Daniel Deronda* used for page references throughout this book is the Everyman (hardback) edition (with an Introduction by A. S. Byatt) published by Everyman, London.

CHAPTER TWO

The Freudian superego

"There is no good father, that's the rule. Don't lay the blame on men but on the bond of paternity, which is rotten . . . Had my father lived, he would have lain on me full length, and would have crushed me . . . I was free to move from shore to shore, alone and hating those invisible begetters who bestraddle their sons all their life long . . .

Was it a good or a bad thing? I don't know. But I readily subscribed to the verdict of an eminent psychoanalyst: I have no superego"

(Jean Paul Sartre as quoted by Lifton, 1993)[1]

"The psychoanalyst 'had unmasked the pretensions of conscience as the perfect guide' "

(Flugel, 1945, p. 33)[2]

The notion of a special part of the mind that had a self-observing, self-judging, and especially self-critical function was present in Freud's early theoretical speculations. For example, in his discussion of defence, repression, and resistance, he describes how an idea that is presented to the mind is forced and kept out of consciousness and out of memory. The process by means of which this threatening idea is kept away from consciousness is referred to as "censorship and censoring" (Freud, 1895d, see pp. 269 and 282 for a description of how censoring works).

As a result of Freud's research into dreams at the turn of the twentieth century, the concept of the censor was further elaborated and related to the process of distortion, in which the latent dream thoughts are disguised by modifications of the dream content. He refers to the censorship as "a second agency", and a psychical force that is powerful, strict, demanding, and dominating. He also describes how the subject comes to dread the censor and how it can sometimes be eluded. In dreams, the censor "forcibly brings about a distortion in the expression of a wish" that seeks consciousness. He further suggests that the motive in this psychic situation is linked to the sexual factor, that certain sexualized ideas seek conscious recognition, but are "forbidden by the censor" (Freud, 1900a, pp. 142–143).[3]

However, at this stage in his explorations of the unconscious, Freud says that the nature of the censor's operation in dreams is unknown to us. He nevertheless associates "the censorship of endopsychic defence" with various kinds of dream work and the influence of resistance, which he says imposes severe conditions upon this work. For example, he describes how the censorship's "objections" are especially well met by means of the creation of composite figures and the use of reversal (i.e., "turning a thing into its opposite") (ibid., p. 327).

The idea of a censoring aspect of the mind was further developed in Freud's classical essay, On narcissism (1914c). In this work, he describes how, as part of normal development and self-preservation, an allocation of "ego libido" is directed to the self and he differentiates this form of libido from that which is invested in an object. He further describes how, in illness, interest may be withdrawn from the object and invested in the self. He says that, in early childhood, an "anaclitic object choice" (i.e., a choice based on a pattern of dependence on someone other than the self) takes place, in that the mother (or mother substitute) becomes the first object on which the child models itself. According to Freud, it is only when this process is disturbed that the child becomes attached to its own self, and models itself as a love object. He refers to this situation as "narcissistic object choice" (i.e., when a person chooses an object on the basis of some real or imagined similarity with himself). Freud describes how libidinal instinctual impulses are "repressed", if they come into conflict with the subject's cultural and ethical ideas and standards that have been derived from the parents and significant others. He says that the subject submits to the claims that these internalized ideals make on him.

It is also in this essay that Freud first introduced the term *ego ideal*, a concept that foreshadowed the superego. He described the ego ideal as the self's conception of how it wishes to be. He further suggested that any aspect of the subject's behaviour that was in conflict with it evoked shame and guilt (Freud, 1914c, p. 93).

Freud uses the term "ego ideal" synonymously with *the ideal ego* and makes no distinction between the two terms (see Laplanche & Pontalis, 1973, for a further discussion of these two terms). He says that one man sets up an ideal in himself by which he measures his actual ego, while another does not. In the first case the *ideal ego* then becomes the target that the self sets up as the model to be sought after. The subject's narcissism is displaced on to this new ego ideal and, like the infantile ego, it is endowed with perfection. He describes how, as development proceeds, the subject becomes more aware and responsive to the criticism of others, so that this perfection cannot be retained.

However, the subject seeks to recover the lost perfection in the new form of an ego ideal, which, according to Freud, becomes "a substitute for the last narcissism of his childhood in which he was his own ideal" (Freud, 1914c, p. 94).

He further suggests that the idealization that is active in relation to an object (e.g., falling in love) can also develop in the sphere of the ego libido and the ego ideal. In a memorable phrase, he comments that "a man may exchange his narcissism for homage to a high ego ideal" (*ibid.*, p. 94).

The concept of the ego ideal and its relationship to the ego is further developed in *Group Psychology and the Analysis of the Ego* (1921c). It is in this essay that Freud introduced the concept of *identification*, which he defines as "the earliest expression of an emotional tie with another person". The concept of identification is crucial for the further understanding of the ego ideal and the theory of the Oedipus complex, which he defines in general terms as "the entire range of feelings the child may experience in relation to his parents and interactions he or she may have with them" (Neu, 1991, p. 161).[4]

Identification involves the developmental process of moulding "a person's own ego after the fashion of the one that has been taken as a model" and this involves the *introjection* of the object into the ego. 2 00

3.25   Freud uses the clinical example of melancholia (i.e., depression) to describe how the ego becomes divided into two parts, one of which rages against the other. He refers to this "cruel" part under various headings (i.e., the ego ideal, the conscience, the critical agency, the censorship) and describes it as the chief influence in repression. He then compares this pathological situation with one in health, in which, although the ego ideal may be critical of the ego, it does not act in such an extreme way. He adds that there are wide individual differences in the relationship between the ego ideal and "the real ego", and he comments further that, for many people in adulthood, the ego ideal will remain at a child-like level.

Freud also links the concept of *idealization* to the ego ideal and he then explores the nature of the two states of mind induced by "being in love" and by hypnosis. He sees the lover as a substitute for the subject's sought after ego ideal (Freud, 1921c, p. 112).

In extreme cases of both object love and the sublimated devotion to an abstract idea, he describes the object as "consuming" the ego. In this instance, the ego ideal's critical functions are silent in that, in the lover's eyes, the loved one can do no wrong. He pointedly observes that, in the love situation, "conscience has no application to anything that is done for the sake of the object" (i.e., because the loved one has been put in the place of the ego ideal). In a further observation, he notes that love of an object also contributes to civilization in that it puts a check on the individual's narcissism.[5]

In his theoretical speculations, Freud comments on the possible variations and combinations that are inherent in the identification process, the ego, the ego ideal, and the object. He describes the complexity involved in the formation of a group (i.e., "the incomprehensible and mysterious in group formations"), and he speculates on the role of the ego ideal in the formation of leader-led groups. He suggests that, in a primary group, the members have replaced their individual ego ideals with the same object, i.e., the leader, and have identified themselves with one another (Freud, 1921c).

In the penultimate section of the essay, he describes a "differentiating grade in the ego" and suggests that each individual, in addition to his independence and originality, constructs his ego ideal upon various models. These may include such group influences as race, class, creed, and nationality. However, he says that, in many persons, the ego and the ego ideal coincide and the ego preserves its earlier narcissistic self-complacency. It is as a result of this process that a leader comes to be selected. He says such a person needs only to possess the typical qualities of the other individuals in a pure form.

He also describes a sense of triumph, when something in the ego coincides with the ideal, and he contrasts this with the opposite experiences of guilt and inferiority, when it does not. It is the non-alignment between the two agencies that produces tension, and he illustrates this with the example of mood swings. He theorizes that "the ego ideal [is] temporarily resolved into [the] ego after having previously ruled it with especial strictness", and he illustrates the relationship between the ego and ego ideal in the states of mania and depression. He says that, in mania, the two agencies are fused so that there is no concern for the feelings of others, whereas, in depression, they are in sharp conflict and this results in a severe attack on the self (*ibid.*, p. 133).

In a further discussion of depression, Freud draws attention to the variety and obscurity of this state of mind, which, he notes, defies any simple explanation. In his summary, he again refers to the complex relationships between the ego, the object, the ego ideal, and the process of identification (*ibid.*, p. 129).

It is in his article *The Ego and the Id* (1923b) that Freud first refers, in a written publication, to the term *superego* (*Uber Ich*, literally, "over the *ego*, the *I*, or the *self*").[6]

In this work, he further develops the ideas on identification referred to above, in that a "superego" arises from a modification of the ego as a result of the child's identification with parental figures. He describes how this change in the ego produces an agency which retains a special position in the psyche in that the modified part of the ego confronts and judges the rest of the ego as a "super"-ego. He refers to the quality of strictness in this agency and further defines it as "the conscious sense of guilt", as experienced by the subject as a "conscience". However, he says that the superego also produces in the subject an "unconscious sense of guilt". The superego has two aspects in so far as it sets a standard or ideal (e.g., "You ought to be like this!"), while at the same time it forbids the subject's choice (e.g., "You may not be like this (like your father)" (Freud, 1923b, p. 34)). 3.30

According to Freud, the superego is formed from the child's first identifications with the parents, which are general and lasting. This formation takes place at the early oedipal stage of the child's development when the ego is still weak. However, in time, although the ego becomes strengthened and modified, the identifications retain their original character and dominating power (Freud, 1923b, p. 29).

The development of this process and its ramifications are described in more detail in the next chapter.

Freud first considers the process of identification at the oedipal stage from the point of view of the little boy and his relationship with the mother. This is one of "primary identification" in that the infant has "a sense of oneness" that is prior to the formation of other relationships. He says that the boy attaches himself to the mother by incorporating the breast, and relates to the father by identification. At a later stage, a simple, "positive Oedipus complex" develops, in which the boy unconsciously experiences a hostile wish to rid himself of the father in order to take his place with the mother. The relationship with the father then continues as an ambivalent one, while that with the mother persists alongside this but is a solely affectionate one.

According to Freud, if development continues along normal-enough lines, the boy's identification with the mother lessens, whereas that with the father is strengthened. In this sense, he speaks of "the dissolution of the Oedipus complex". However, he also says that, if the boy's feminine disposition is strong, his development may proceed in identification with the mother.

Freud's account of the little girl's development is described along similar lines, but with a reversal of the patterns of identification. On the one hand, she may resolve her Oedipal situation by means

of an intensification of identification with the mother and a relin-
quishing of the strong attachment to the father. On the other hand,
if the girl has a strong masculine disposition, she may react to the
loss of attachment to the father by a continuing identification
with him.

Applying his theory of bisexuality, Freud further describes a
more complicated and complete pattern of the Oedipus complex,
which combines positive (normal) and negative (inverted) features.
In the negative situation, the boy displays an affectionate, "feminine" attitude to his father and shows more hostile feelings to the
mother, whereas the girl experiences the opposite set of feelings
(Freud, 1923b, p. 33).

The resolution of the Oedipus complex is described in broad
developmental terms in which two sets of identifications unite with
each other. The superego's confrontation with the ego has a double
aspect in that it is a residue of the earliest object choices of the id, but
it is also an "energetic reaction formation" against those choices in
that it had the task of repressing the Oedipus complex.

According to Freud, it is in this way that the superego retains the
character of the father. In the course of development, a relationship
is formed in which the power of the early superego and the speed of
its repression are related to its later strictness and its dominance over
the ego. At the more conscious level, this power may become mani-
fest as conscience but, at a greater depth, it produces "an unconscious
sense of guilt". This whole process is summarized in the well-known
phrase, "the superego is the heir of the Oedipus complex".

In this essay, Freud goes on to describe how the differentiation
of the superego from the ego speaks to humanity's "higher nature"
(i.e., its morality), and how it is highly significant for the individual
and the species in that it gives a "permanent expression to the influence of the parents".

He also describes the deeply unconscious aspects of the superego. Since it is always close to the id, it can express its most powerful impulses and acts as the id's representative *vis-à-vis* the ego. He
notes that the superego reaches deep down into the id (for its
energy) and is further from consciousness than the ego. Since, in
contrast to the ego, the superego represents the internal world of
the id, the conflicts between the ego and the superego ultimately
reflect those between the external and the internal world.

Freud concludes that the supreme importance of the superego lies in its origin, in which the "lowest" primitive parts of mental life are gradually changed into the "highest" civilized values. It is, in this sense, that he notes its significance for the establishment of civilization (Freud, 1923b, p. 37).

In considering the dependent relationships of the ego, he describes how the superego, though first established at a time when the ego was weak and dependent, nevertheless continues to assert its "categorical imperative" on the mature ego, which therefore remains subject to its domination (*ibid.*, p. 48).

Freud finds support for his superego theory in the clinical evidence of the "negative therapeutic reaction", in which the patient's resistance to recovery results from a masochistic wish to suffer. This reaction arises, according to Freud, from the unconscious sense of guilt referred to above. He points out how this finds its satisfaction in illness and refuses to give up punishment, and how it is also "dumb". The patient, he says, "does not feel guilty, he feels ill", and Freud claims that unconscious guilt expresses itself as a resistance to recovery. He describes the "difficult" task of the analyst, which is that of changing unconscious into conscious guilt, and he notes that success in this task may depend on the intensity of the unconscious guilt and also on the personality of the analyst (i.e., the capacity to resist the invitation to play the part of prophet, saviour, etc.).

Freud describes how the nature and quality of the superego (exemplified by the way the unconscious sense of guilt expresses itself) determine the severity of a neurotic illness. He defines the normal, conscious sense of guilt as "the tension between the ego and the ego ideal" and suggests that, when it becomes "over-strongly conscious" and reaches extraordinary strength, it may give rise, for example, to obsessional neurosis and/or melancholia.

In both of these pathological states, he comments that the superego is very severe and cruelly attacks the ego. However, he also points to important differences between the two states of mind. In the obsessional, he describes the sense of guilt as "over-noisy" and the superego as being under the influence of processes that remain unknown to the ego. In graphic terms, he describes how, when the repressed impulses are responsible for the sense of guilt, the superego knows "more than the ego about the unconscious id".

In contrast, he says, in melancholia, the superego has obtained a hold on consciousness and the ego feels guilty and accepts punishment. According to Freud, this is because "the object to which the superego's wrath applies has been taken into the ego through identification". I shall now consider some case material in relation to these ideas.

Case study: Mrs Blue

To illustrate Freud's distinction between conscious and unconscious guilt, I draw on some clinical material from a patient whose superego punished her ego to an extent that resulted in prolonged physical and mental suffering. In this case, the analytic process was able to achieve a limited change in her social functioning, although evidence of a more structural modification in her internal situation was less clear.

> Mrs Blue was a very intelligent, energetic, and tough-minded woman who had sought my help in middle age. The early phase of treatment was dominated by strong feelings of anger and resentment about the undeserved blows that were the result of her "fate" in life. Her overwhelming anger about this seems to have been incorporated into her body, which had reacted with recurring patterns of painful, physical symptoms. In the analysis, she described her early prematurity and her mother's difficulties in bonding in a situation in which she (the patient) was not expected to survive. She had then experienced a further profound loss in early childhood, when her much loved father died. This event had marked the end for her of "a golden age", and this was further worsened with the replacement by a hated step-father at the time of her adolescent development. She seemed, nevertheless, to have been an example of an outstanding "survivor" in the face of the problems in her life. In the analysis, her concerns were with the unreliability of her body, her struggle to fulfil her academic potential, and, above all, the inability of her family and friends to meet her emotional needs. In spite of a certain idealization of the analyst, these failures were reproduced in that her expectations of the analytic situation could not be met. Her resentment at her "fate" continued to be transformed, either into unconscious attacks on her body (i.e., attacks on an internal object), or verbal criticism of her loved ones, or by extension, to "Destiny", perceived unconsciously as a kind of overall, relentlessly punitive superego.

My interpretative efforts were centred mainly (though not wholly) on the transference, and attempted to shift Mrs Blue's focus from the external world to her internal situation. This seemed to me to be one of extensive unconscious guilt, which had resulted in intensive and prolonged self-punishment. She gradually responded to my interventions by becoming less of a "doormat" in her life, and in finding ways to greater self-fulfilment and freedom to engage in "a life of her own". Nevertheless, these shifts were "limited" by a powerful negative therapeutic reaction (e.g., the cutting down of sessions and an early termination).[7]

In terms of the present discussion, Mrs Blue's psychopathology can be understood as a result of a weakened and helpless ego's attempt to respond to the orders of a particularly critical and punitive superego. The internal situation seemed to reflect her pre-oedipal and oedipal unconscious guilt, which had led to the life-long tendency to self-punishment.

In this example, I have tried to illustrate how, in latent depression (with psychosomatic features), a strongly developed superego had obtained a tight hold on consciousness and the ego, and how this had led to chronic self-punishment.

Freud also applied superego theory to the state of hysteria, in which the sense of guilt remains unconscious. When the superego threatens the hysterical ego with criticism, it responds with an act of repression and the ego is thus itself responsible for the unconscious guilt. In this way, it has succeeded in keeping at a distance the material to which the sense of guilt refers.

Case study of Gwendolen Harleth in Daniel Deronda

To illustrate this process in a (fictionalized) hysterical personality, I shall describe George Eliot's heroine, Gwendolen Harleth, in her novel *Daniel Deronda*, a summary of which is provided at the end of Chapter One. Gwendolen is a twenty-one year-old, described as clever, beautiful, vivacious, and as a "princess in exile". However, she is also strikingly flawed in that her immaturity, ignorance, and egotism tend to severely narrow her horizons. In addition, her ruthless demand for gratification and a quest for power over others (which take little account of reality) lead her to enter a disastrous marriage, which ends in tragic circumstances.

In the course of the action, the hysterical features of her personality are exposed by means of a series of memorable events and episodes. For example, when one of her four half-sisters accidentally causes a wall panel to fly open, revealing a picture of a dead face and a fleeing figure, Eliot vividly describes Gwendolen's response as follows :

> [there was] . . . a piercing cry from Gwendolen who stood . . . with a change of expression that was terrifying in its terror . . . a soul of fear had entered: her pallid lips were parted . . . her eyes dilated and fixed.

She responds to her cousin, Rex's, expressions of love (which are unwelcome to her) not with a simple rejection, but with an agitation that suggests a terror of being touched: " 'Pray don't make love to me. I hate it . . .' [and she] looked at him fiercely", and later, in conversation with her mother, she refers to the problem that she has with loving feelings: "I shall never love anybody. I can't love people. I hate them . . . I can't bear anyone to be near me but you".

We are also told of Gwendolen's "nervous susceptibilities", which include the fear of being alone, of changes in the daylight, and of large open spaces. However, it is in her marriage that the "nervous disorders" have the most profound impact. Threatened by poverty and its implications, she has sought security for herself, her mother, and her sisters, in a loveless marriage. Her husband, Grandcourt, is a man "with a withered heart" and is incapable of sympathetic feeling. He is significantly more narcissistic than Gwendolen and is gratified only by his power over others, including his wife.

In another episode, Gwendolen, on her wedding night, receives a package of jewels ("poisonous gems") from her husband's former mistress, which also contains a threatening letter. When Grandcourt appears in her room, Eliot writes: "She screamed again and again with hysterical violence . . . He saw her pallid face shrieking as it seemed with terror . . . was it a fit of madness? . . . the furies had crossed his threshold".

As the marriage deteriorates, Gwendolen's cumulative hate for her husband becomes an unconscious death wish, and this is fulfilled when he is accidentally drowned. This event brings her hidden murderous thoughts to consciousness, and this has a profound effect on her conscience.

I return now to further discussion of *The Ego and the Id*, in which Freud describes how criminals may commit crimes "to obtain relief" from an "unconscious sense of guilt", which had existed *before* the crime. The crime, then, is an action done to obtain relief. He also observes that "the normal man is not only far more immoral than he believes, but also far more moral than he knows". Human nature, he says, has, to a far greater extent, a tendency for both good and evil than it thinks it has (Freud, 1923b, p. 52).

He also considers the question of how the superego obtains its energy by referring to the "sources in the id" from which it develops its extraordinary harshness and severity towards the ego.

In the example of melancholia, Freud now introduces into the discussion "the pure culture of the death instinct". The superego acts sadistically because it represents the death instinct and may, therefore, even succeed in "driving the ego to death". He distinguishes the id as a totally non-moral agency, from the ego's moral strivings, and from the cruel, "super"-morality of the superego.

Freud compares the findings of psychoanalytic research with the conventional viewpoint that an individual suppresses his aggression by setting and following standards and ideals. He says, "the more a man controls his aggressiveness, the more intense becomes his ideal's inclination to aggressiveness against his ego. It is like a displacement, a turning round upon his own ego" (*ibid.*, p. 54).

In an attempt to explain how this happens, he introduces a new hypothesis. He first restates how the source of the superego lies in identification with the father and then says that this transformation is accompanied by a "diffusion" of the erotic and destructive instincts. Thus, the desexualization that is involved in the identification process weakens the erotic instinct's function of "binding", and it is this that releases the destructive forces. These forces provide the source of the superego's dictatorial powers, its "Thou shalt" (*ibid.*, pp. 54–55).

Freud considers that the ego is menaced and threatened from three directions, i.e., the external world, the id, and the superego. The ego's work of sublimation results in a defusion of the instincts and a "liberation of the aggressive instincts in the superego", a process that contributes to its severity and its cruelty. The ego then stands in a dependent relationship to the superego and "dreads" it. The term *Gewissensangst*, "the fear of conscience", is used to describe this dread. He also considers what is hidden behind the ego's dread of the superego. He says that the superior being that has been turned into the ego ideal "once threatened castration and this dread of castration is probably the nucleus round which the subsequent fear of conscience gathered, it is this dread that persists as the fear of conscience" (*ibid.*, p. 57).

For the individual ego, "living" is equivalent to "being loved by the superego", which is also representing the id, and Freud notes that "the superego fulfils the same function of protecting and saving that was fulfilled in earlier days by the father and later by Providence or Destiny" (*ibid.*, p. 58).

However, in a further reference to melancholia (in which the ego finds itself helpless "when it is in excessive real danger, feels abandoned, surrenders" and "lets itself die"), he makes an important addition. He says that this desertion results in "separation anxiety", and that this is akin to abandonment by the protecting mother.

In concluding this essay, Freud draws attention to the associations among the fear of death, the fear of conscience, and the fear of castration. He now suggests that the great significance of the sense of guilt in the neuroses results from the generating of anxiety between the ego and the superego.

In an essay published a few years later, *Inhibitions, Symptoms and Anxiety* (1926d), Freud outlines the crucial role of anxiety in the neuroses. He defines an "inhibition" as the expression of a restriction, or loss of an ego function, a kind of holding in check. The inhibiting agency is either the ego or the superego, which he says "switches something off".

He distinguishes an inhibition from a symptom in that the former is an "expression of a restriction of an ego function" and the latter necessarily denotes "some pathological process". A symptom is "a substitute for an instinctual satisfaction which has remained in abeyance" because of repression (i.e., it holds something back).

He then goes on to expand on how the loss of the superego's love (i.e., its severity) poses a threat to the ego that may result in a sense of guilt and consequent self-punishment (e.g., in melancholia). An inhibition can serve the purpose of self-punishment in so far as the superego may forbid a certain activity and the ego, to avoid conflict, gives up the activity, as in the example of the phobias. 8.03

In this essay, Freud returns to the problem of the ego, and lays stress on its complexity, its strength, and the quality of its organization. He says that, although in one respect the act of repression reveals the ego's powerlessness, it also demonstrates its strength, in that it shows how it gains control of the path to action and of the access to consciousness (Freud, 1926d, p. 97).

The ego, he says, is identified with the id and is a differentiated part of it. Its strength is maintained in so far as it merges with the id as its "organized portion". In respect of this organizing power, he emphasizes the ego's binding, unifying, and synthesizing qualities. He then describes the example of its role in hysterical symptoms in establishing a compromise formation (*ibid.*, pp. 98–99).

In relation to the superego, there is a similar merging with the ego. Freud says, "We can only distinguish one from the other when there is a tension or conflict between them". He returns to another consideration of obsessional neurosis and notes that the ego and the superego play a large part in the formation of the symptoms. He comments that the obsessional's superego is exceptionally severe and unkind, and the ego, "in obedience to it", produces strong reaction formations in the shape of conscientiousness, pity, and cleanliness. He also suggests that the severity of the superego may be due to the regression of the libido to anal–sadistic concerns.

In introducing his speculative essay, *The Future of an Illusion* (1927c), Freud begins with some reflections on the nature of culture. In essence, he argues that human survival and the development of civilization depend on the renunciation of primitive instinctual wishes such as incest, cannibalism, and "lust for killing". He gives an account of what he will later refer to as "the cultural superego", and he stresses its role and significance as a coercive agency, although one that also helps to enforce the rules of civilized behaviour. In this paper, he also describes the role of the superego in the development of the human mind from its primitive origins in early childhood. For Freud, the transformation of the superego and its internalization is a precious cultural asset and the vehicle of civilization. He says:

> [in] the course of human development external coercion gradually
> becomes internalized; for a special mental agency, man's superego,

takes it over and includes it among its commandments. Every child presents this process of transformation to us; only by this means does it become a moral and social being. Such a strengthening of the superego is a most precious cultural asset in the psychological field. Those in whom it has taken place are turned from being opponents of civilization into being its vehicles. The greater their number is in a cultural unit, the more secure is its culture and the more it can dispense with external measures of coercion. [*ibid.,* p. 11]

These ideas are further expanded by Freud in his well-known work, *Civilization and its Discontents* (1930a). The main theme of this essay is "the irremediable antagonism" between instinctual demands and the restrictions imposed upon "civilized" man. He seeks to demonstrate how an excess of these restrictions can result in a kind of instinctual backlash, and sets out to describe the relationship between the internal civilizing factors and the external influences. In his description of this relationship, his theory of the superego plays a central role.

He also describes the positive role of the sense of guilt in the growth of civilization, and in relation to the darker forces in the human situation, i.e., the destructive tendencies in the psyche. He poses the question as to how this aggression is opposed, inhibited, and rendered harmless, and he describes the process in which it is internalized and turned upon the self (*ibid.,* p. 123).

Building on his earlier formulations of the sense of guilt, he describes how this expresses itself as a need for punishment, and suggests that its origin belongs to the stage of helplessness and dependency in early childhood when the child experiences a fear of punishment and loss of love. He refers to this fear as social anxiety, which he also associates with the popular notion of the bad conscience.

Freud contrasts this idea of an external reference point with that of a new, internal authority that is established in the self (i.e., the superego). He suggests that only when this acquisition is firmly established can we accurately speak of conscience and a (conscious) sense of guilt. He goes on to describe how the "authority" of the superego is established by means of the gradual gains in its strength and sphere of influence and how, as a result of this developmental process, the distinction between doing something bad and wishing to do it disappears. He concludes that, since the super-ego equates thoughts and actions, nothing can be hidden from it (Freud, 1940a, p. 125).

To illustrate some of these ideas, I return to *Daniel Deronda*. In the novel, the heroine, Gwendolen, equates and thereby confuses and exaggerates her thoughts and actions. This is most clearly illustrated when she is caught up in the incident in which her husband accidently drowns. In the novel, we learn that, in the course of her growth and development, she has been affected by, and become terrified of, powerful, murderous, unconscious wishes. These are first experienced in adolescence towards her four half-siblings (for example, in a fit of pique, she strangles her sister's canary). At another level, I would suggest that these wishes are fuelled by deeper hostile and guilt feelings connected with the father who died when she was very young. It is in later life that these impulses are acted out, when, in the boating accident, Gwendolen "hesitates" to make an attempt to rescue the husband that she hates. After Grandcourt's death, she is in a state of high agitation and, when confessing her guilt feelings to Daniel, she describes how her conscience is severely punishing her.

> . . . But I did, I did kill him in my thoughts . . . evil wishes were too strong . . . and blotted everything else dim . . . he was struck . . . I know nothing . . . I only know that I saw my wish outside me . . . I think I did not move . . . my heart said "Die!" [however . . .] I would have saved him then.

In fact, it is at this point that she actually jumps into the sea and makes an unsuccessful rescue attempt. This utterance is a good illustration of Freud's statement of how the superego torments the "sinful" ego and searches for opportunities to get it punished.

In considering and responding to her story, Daniel comments:

> The word "guilty" had held a possibility of interpretations worse than the fact; . . . [and] her conscience made her dwell on the determining power of her evil thoughts [even though . . .] the death was inevitable. Still . . . the outward effectiveness of a criminal desire dominant enough to impel even a momentary act, cannot alter our judgment of the desire. . . . Gwendolen's remorse aggravated her inward guilt.

In *Civilization and its Discontents*, Freud suggests that the sense of guilt (i.e., "permanent internal unhappiness") has two sources: the first lies in the "infantile stage" of conscience and its fear of authority, and the second in the fear of the later established superego. The first demands the giving up of instinctual satisfactions and the second "presses" for self-punishment, since the forbidden wishes cannot be hidden from the superego (1930a, p. 127).

He turns next to consider the severity of the superego, and begins his discussion by describing it as a continuation of the severity of the external authority. He shows, however, that the internal authority differs in an important respect in that, although there may be a renunciation of instinctual acts, the wishes may remain intact and are observed by the superego, which equates bad intentions with bad actions. This situation, he says, leads to "a permanent internal unhappiness . . . the tension of the sense of guilt" (*ibid.*, p. 128).

Freud now deals with what he calls a "peculiarity" of conscience, namely that "good" men may nevertheless suffer disproportionate pangs of guilt, and he considers why it is that the severity of conscience comes to be sustained even in the face of virtue. He points out how a paradoxical situation develops in that a virtuous, even saintly, man may, in his mind, suffer a severely distrustful superego which leads to punishing self-reproaches.

He seeks an answer to this paradox in the cumulative effects of instinctual renunciation. He says:

> Every renunciation of instinct now becomes a dynamic source of conscience, and every fresh renunciation increases the latter's severity and intolerance. [*ibid.*, p. 128]

> . . . every piece of agression whose satisfaction the subject gives up is taken over by the superego and increases the latter's agressiveness (against the ego). [*ibid.*, p. 129]

Freud also returns to the theme of the role of identification in the formation of the superego. It is the means by which the "unattackable [external] authority" is taken into the self and turned into the superego. With this internalization, the superego inherits the aggressiveness that was originally directed against the external authority. The severity, therefore, of the superego "represents" the child's own suppressed aggressiveness, and this severity may not reflect the actual attitude and behaviour of the parents towards the child. In this connection, he notes that "a child that has been very leniently brought up can acquire a very strict conscience". However, he also acknowledges that a strict upbringing in itself may also have a strong influence. He says:

> ... in the formation of a superego and the emergence of a conscience innate constitutional factors and influences from the real environment act in combination ... a severe conscience arises from the joint operation of two factors: the frustration of instinct, which unleashes aggressiveness, and the experience of being loved, which turns the aggressiveness inwards and hands it over to the superego. [*ibid.*, p. 130]

In further considering the origin of the sense of guilt, Freud cites the Oedipus complex and the killing of the primeval father by the band of brothers, which was, he says, "a case of remorse" (Freud, 1912–1913). He then considers the relationship between remorse and what he calls "the fatal inevitability" of the sense of guilt. He argues that remorse only applies to a deed that has been carried out and suggests further that it is only in this case:

> the feeling should ... be called remorse ... [which] presupposes that a conscience—the readiness to feel guilty—was already in existence before the deed took place. Remorse ... can, therefore, never help us to discover the origin of conscience and of the sense of guilt in general. [1930a, p. 131]

Returning to the killing of the primal father by the brothers and their remorse, he emphasizes the part played by love. He says:

> the remorse was the result of the ambivalence of feeling towards the father. His sons hated him but they loved him too [and] ... the love comes to the fore in their remorse after the killing. [*ibid.*, p. 132]

He understands this process as reinforced by every piece of repressed aggressiveness that was suppressed and carried over into the superego (*ibid.*, p. 132).

Freud, therefore, concludes that the sense of guilt arises as an expression of the ambivalence generated by the struggle between the life and death instincts. This conflict expresses itself in the Oedipus complex and the ever-increasing reinforcement of the sense of guilt. He says:

> If civilization is a necessary course of development from the family to humanity . . . then as a result of the conflict arising from ambivalence . . . of the struggle between . . . love and death—there is inextricably bound up with it an increase of the sense of guilt, which will perhaps reach heights that the individual finds hard to tolerate . . . [*ibid.*, p. 133]

In the last part of the paper, Freud reaffirms his view that the sense of guilt is produced by civilization and is the most important problem in its development. The advance in civilization depends on a heightening of the consciousness of the sense of guilt, for which humanity pays a price. In this respect, he once more cites the clinical evidence of obsessional neurosis, in which the sense of guilt is central and is consciously experienced. He further describes the sense of guilt as a type of anxiety which coincides with "fear of the superego".

He then attempts a clarification and more specific use of terms that hitherto he has tended to use interchangeably. He says that the superego is a critical agency and that conscience is a function of that agency. The superego's task is to watch over the ego, judge it, and censor it. He equates sense of guilt, harshness of the superego and severity of conscience. All these, he says, are underpinned by the need for punishment. He also considers the concept of remorse as a general term for the ego's reaction in a case of a conscious sense of guilt. However, in a more specific sense, he suggests limiting the use of the concept of remorse to the situation of a conscious feeling that may be experienced after an aggressive action has actually been carried out.

He continues this discussion by considering these concepts in terms of the relations between the ego, id, and superego. He describes the ego as becoming masochistic when influenced by the sadistic superego and he suggests that the idea of conscience depends on the presence of a superego. However, he considers that both the sense of guilt and remorse exist prior to this development of conscience, since they depend on fear of external authority. The sense of guilt, then, has two strata, which are superimposed on each other: the fear of external authority and the fear of internal authority (*ibid.*, p. 137).

Freud next considers the influence of the superego on the cultural development of a community. He says that its cultural origin is similar to that of an individual and that its manifestations and properties are accessible to observation in the community.

> It is based on the impression left behind by the personalities of great leaders, men of overwhelming force of mind or men in whom one of the human impulsions has found its strongest and purest, and, therefore, often its most one-sided, expression. [*ibid.*, p. 141]

As in the individual case, *the cultural superego* advances strict standards and demands, which, if disobeyed, set off the fear of conscience. Among these demands is "ethics", which concerns the relations of persons to one another. An example of such a demand is the ethical commandment to "love one's neighbour as oneself". However, Freud considers this commandment impossible to fulfil, because he says it is based on the erroneous assumption that a person's ego "has unlimited mastery over his id".

Lastly, Freud extends the analogy between individual and cultural development in order to suggest the idea of "neurotic epochs" of civilization (i.e., '"communal neurosis"). Although he notes certain problems with this extension, he nevertheless suggests that further investigation into "a pathology of cultural communities" is a possibility for future research.

In 1933, Freud reviewed and summarized his superego research in his inappropriately titled article, *New Introductory Lectures On Psychoanalysis* (1933a). This review was carried out in the light of the deepening knowledge and critical revisions of psychoanalytic theory.

He begins this article from the well-established premise that a part of the ego becomes separated from the whole and functions as an observing agency within the ego.

The first of these superego functions is to observe the ego, which, he says, is a preparation for other functions such as judging the ego and punishing it. All these are associated with the idea of the voice of conscience, and this he links with punishing self-reproaches and with remorse.

In relation to the ego, the superego has a certain degree of autonomy, in that it goes its own way and has an independent supply of
energy. He then illustrates the nature of superego functioning once
more with the example of melancholia. In this condition, he says,
we can observe the superego's severity, its cruelty, and its changing
situation in relation to the ego. In melancholia, the superego
becomes:

> ... over-severe, abuses the poor ego, humiliates it and ill-treats it,
> threatens it with the direst punishments, reproaches it for actions in
> the remotest past ... [it] applies the strictest moral standard to the
> helpless ego which is at its mercy; in general it represents the claims
> of morality [*ibid.*, p. 61].

He compares this victory of the superego with that of its opposite, manic behaviour, in which the ego celebrates a triumph over
the superego, which, in this situation, has lost its strength.
He discusses the origin of the superego in relation to religious belief
and finds it not in God, but, as described in previous work,
in the external authority of the parents. This authority is based on
"... proofs of love and ... threatening punishments" (which
are feared as "loss of love"). This "real fear" (i.e., derived from a
reaction to the external world) is the precursor of the later "moral
anxiety" (*Gewissensangst*, literally, *conscience anxiety*), which has
been internalized and becomes fear of the superego.

He describes the established superego as having taken over the
parents' prohibitive and punitive function, but not their loving care.
This is the case even when the parents' care has been benign, mild,
and kindly (*ibid.*, p. 62). However, he also notes that the transformation of the external parental agency into the internal superego is
a complicated matter, not completely understood, and can therefore
only be sketched in outline.

He continues with another account of the identification process
in which one ego comes to resemble another: "the first ego behaves
like the second in certain respects, imitates it and in a sense takes it
up into itself" (i.e., the boy modelling himself on the father has
become like him). This identification process differs from object
choice in so far as the boy wants to be like his father rather than to
possess him. In the case of object loss (the loss of a person), the
subject often compensates by identifying with the lost object and

setting it up once more in the ego. This is a regressive process from object choice to identification with the earliest parental imagoes (*ibid*, p. 63).

The superego, says Freud, is linked with the destiny of the Oedipus complex, it is "the heir of that [childhood] emotional attachment". The process consists of the child's renunciation of the intense feelings towards the parents, which results in the strengthening and intensification of the identifications with them. The superego, he says, remains stunted in its strength and growth if this process is incomplete. During the life cycle, the process of identification is increasingly influenced by other figures of authority such as educators, teachers, and idealized persons, and by this means the superego comes to be more and more impersonalized.

In this article, Freud seeks to distinguish the *superego* from *conscience* in that he suggests that the origin of the former involves a structural modification of the mind, whereas he refers to conscience as "a mere personification of . . . [an] abstraction".

He also distinguishes the *superego* from the *ego ideal* in that the former is the "vehicle" of the ideal "by which the ego measures itself, which it emulates, and whose demand for ever greater perfection it strives to fulfil" (*ibid.*, p. 65). The ego ideal is the precipitate of the child's image of perfection, and the superego is the "enforcing agency".

Freud next takes up the issue of the roots of the "sense of inferiority", which he relates to the ego's relation to the superego. He says that, as in the case of the sense of guilt, inferiority is a product of the tension between the two (*ibid.*, p. 66).

In his discussion, he turns next to "the higher side of human life" and notes that, since the superego is the source of all moral restrictions and strives for perfection, the influence of parents and other authorities are of crucial importance in its formation. He says, they, the parents,

> follow the precepts of their own superegos in educating children. . . . They are severe and exacting [and] they identify themselves fully with their own (previously severely restricting) parents. . . . Thus a child's superego is in fact constructed on the model not of its parents, but of its parents' superego; the contents which fill it are the same and it becomes the vehicle of tradition . . . and of the

[permanent] judgements of value [handed down] . . . from generation to generation. [*ibid*., p. 67]

He notes that the superego also helps us to understand social behaviour in that past values and traditions live on in its "ideologies".

He considers next the role of the superego in other psychological processes. For example, in the formation of leader-led human
groups, the group may be defined with reference to the superego
and the leader:

> . . . A psychological group is a collection of individuals who have
> introduced the same person into their superego and, on the basis of
> this common element, have identified themselves with another in
> their ego. [*ibid*., p. 69]

In relation to the unconscious process of defence, he says that,
since repression can be recognized as "the work of the superego",
either carried out by itself or by the ego in obedience to it, we can
conclude that both the ego and the superego are partly unconscious
(i.e., "they are normally unconscious and remain unconscious") in
the dynamic sense.

He describes the ego as serving the superego and the id, each of
which it tries to obey simultaneously, while at the same time taking
into account the demands of reality ("the external world"). In this
situation, the superego sets the standards for the ego's conduct,
observes it, and, if the standards are not reached, severely punishes
it with feelings of inferiority and guilt.

In this article, Freud discusses the superego in its relation to
anxiety. He says the ego is the sole seat of signal anxiety and it alone
"produces and feels anxiety" (*ibid*., p. 85). It is when under pressure
from the id, the superego, and the external world that the ego reacts
with anxiety. He describes types of anxiety as *neurotic, moral,* and
realistic with respect to each of these agencies. He also considers the
concept of anxiety from a developmental point of view and notes
that the precursor of the superego in infancy is associated with the
fear of loss of (parental) love ("social anxiety"). Later, at the latency
stage, the ego's fear of the superego ("moral anxiety"), he says,
"assumes a special position". This fear, which is crucial to social
relationships, "should normally never cease".

He also considers the superego from the structural point of view, and says that, in relation to the id, there is a merger. Also, as the heir to the Oedipus complex, the superego becomes closely attached to the large and powerful id, and is more remote from the perceptual system than is the case with the ego. Freud considers that the differentiation between the ego and the superego is phylo-genetically the "last and most delicate" of the divisions of the mind and is subject to temporary entanglement.

According to Freud, the mental situation that he describes has important implications for the aims of therapy (aims which coincide with the promotion of "culture"). In an interesting statement, he says that these aims are "to strengthen the ego, to make it more independent than the superego, to widen its field of perception and enlarge its organisation, so that it can appropriate fresh portions of the id. Where id was, there ego shall be" (*ibid.*, p. 80).

In his discussion of "character", Freud gives an important and decisive role to the superego (*ibid.*, p. 91), and to identifications with the parents and, at a later stage of development, with other influential figures. To this he adds the "reaction formations" (development of an exaggerated opposite tendency to the impulse that the ego finds unacceptable) which take place as a result of repression and the rejection, or transforming, of unwished-for instinctual impulses.

Freud speaks of the *unconscious need for punishment*, and subsequent neurotic suffering, as having a share in every mental illness, and as the worst enemy of therapeutic effort. In this respect he notes:

> . . . it behaves like a piece of conscience, like a prolongation of our conscience and it must have the same origin as conscience and correspond therefore to a piece of aggressiveness that has been internalised and taken over by the superego . . . an unconscious sense of guilt. [*ibid.*, p. 109]

He also links the unconscious sense of guilt with the problem of the *negative therapeutic reaction* in psychotherapy and its connections with morality, education, crime, and delinquency (see *The Ego and the Id* (1923b), *The Economic Problem of Masochism* (1924c), and *Civilization and its Discontents* (1930a)).

Finally, in this article, he returns to the problem of the aggressive instincts that threaten the survival of human life, and notes that the taming of this "unruly thing" is achieved by: ". . . the superego which takes over the dangerous impulses, introduces a garrison as it were into regions that are inclined to rebellion". However, he also notes the ego's unhappiness at "being sacrificed to the needs of society" (*ibid.*, p. 110).

In a section entitled "Femininity" (1933a), Freud describes the little girl's entry to the Oedipus complex as the outcome of a long and difficult development. This takes place in a process that is opposite to that of the boy, in that the castration complex prepares for the Oedipus complex instead of destroying it. He says:

> . . . the girl is driven out of her attachment to her mother through the influence of her envy for the penis and she enters the Oedipus situation as though into a haven of refuge . . . [and remains] in it for an indeterminate length of time; . . . [demolishing] it late and . . . incompletely. [*ibid.*, p. 129]

The implication of this developmental situation is that the female superego suffers. and he famously (infamously?) concludes that it is less strong and independent than the male superego, and that this affects "the average feminine character". A further discussion and critique of this viewpoint can be found in Chapters Three, Four, and Six.

In a discussion of the problem of a *Weltanschauung* (i.e., a comprehensive world view that aims to solve life's problems), Freud comments on the relationship between economic factors and the superego. He says the superego ". . . represents tradition and the ideals of the past and will for a time resist the incentives of a new economic situation". He also insists on the independence of the process of cultural development (i.e., civilization) from "economic necessities" (*ibid.*, p. 242).

In his article, *A disturbance of memory on the Acropolis* (1936a), Freud discusses persons who may fall ill because of a sense of guilt or inferiority and who cannot permit themselves happiness. In these cases, he says: ". . . the Fate which we expect to treat us so badly is a materialization of our conscience, of the severe superego within us, itself a residue of the punitive agency of our childhood" (p. 243).

Freud's last, and unfinished, work is *An outline of psychoanalysis* (1940a), which was written in 1938, but posthumously published. In his introduction, Strachey notes that this essay was "a fascinating epilogue" to Freud's overall theoretical views and threw "new light on whatever he touched" (Strachey, 1964, p. 143).

In this last work, Freud also gives his final account of superego theory, and this is summarized below.

In a return to earlier descriptions, he refers to a special agency that is the result of the child's long dependence on his parents, as a precipitate formed within the ego. In so far as this agency is differentiated from the ego, or is opposed to it, it constitutes a *third power*. It is the ego's task to meet and reconcile the demands made upon it by the id, the system superego, and external reality, but also to preserve and maintain its own autonomy.

Freud notes that the parental influence on the subject extends to family, racial, and national traditions, and to the immediate social milieu. Later, this basic superego system is further developed and sustained by others, such as teachers and "models in public life of admired social ideals". The superego then represents the influence from the past ("essentially of what is taken over from other people").

He clarifies a main function of the superego as the limitation of the instinctual satisfactions for which the ego strives. However, when the superego is established, a large amount of aggression becomes fixed within the ego and Freud notes that this can then operate upon *the self* in a destructive way. Thus, the superego may come to act against the mental health of the individual. Its unconscious demands (reinforced from the id) may become so strong that they cause a paralysis of the ego, an altering of its organization, and this in turn may then lead to a disturbance of the ego's relation to reality or even lead to death.

In a section on technique in relation to the transference, Freud comments on the therapeutic value of the patient's perception of the analyst as a parent figure. It is via the transference relationship that the psychoanalyst may become endowed with the power and authority that the superego exercises over the patient's ego. This has significant implications for the work and aims of the analyst, since this power can be used as a therapeutic tool in the service of the ego. The strategic aim in analysis then becomes one of opposing the superego's demands, and thereby strengthening the weakened ego and helping it to obtain the lost mastery over the subject's mental life.

In a discussion of the sense of guilt (consciousness of guilt), Freud repeats his earlier observation that there is hidden guilt that the patient is not consciously aware of (he does not "feel" it). When the superego becomes particularly severe and cruel to the ego, the accompanying guilt may "insist", so to speak, on the patient remaining ill and in a state of suffering (Freud, 1940a, p. 180). The analyst's task then becomes one of bringing about the "slow demolition" of the superego's power.

In his comment on the child's psychical achievement by the age of five years, Freud provides a final, concise, summary statement of the role and function of the superego, from which I quote selectively:

> A portion of the external world has at least partially been abandoned as an object and has instead by identification been taken into the ego . . .

> This new agency continues to carry on the functions which have hitherto been performed by the people (the abandoned objects) in the external world: it observes the ego, gives it orders, judges it and threatens it with punishments, exactly like the parents whose place it has taken. We call this agency the *superego* and are aware of it in its judicial functions as our *conscience*. It is a remarkable thing that the superego often displays a severity for which no model has been provided by the real parents, and moreover that it calls the ego to account not only for its deeds but equally for its thoughts and unexecuted intentions, of which the superego seems to have knowledge. . . . The superego is in fact the heir to the Oedipus complex and is only established after that complex has been disposed of. For that reason its excessive severity does not follow a real model but corresponds to the strength of the defence used against the temptation of the Oedipus complex. [*ibid.*, p. 205]

Freud concludes:

> the torments caused by the reproaches of conscience correspond precisely to a child's fear of loss of love, a fear the place of which has been taken by the moral agency. On the other hand, if the ego has successfully resisted a temptation to do something which would be objectionable to the superego, it feels raised in its self-esteem and strengthened in its pride. . . . In this way the superego continues to play the part of an external world for the ego although it has become part of the internal world. . . . It is not only the

personal qualities of these parents that is making itself felt, but also everything that had a determining effect on them themselves ... the social class ... the traditions of the race ... For those who have a liking for generalisations ... the superego represents ... the cultural past ... much of what is contributed by the superego will awaken an echo in the id.

Thus the superego takes up a kind of intermediate position between the id and the external world; it unites in itself the influences of the present and the past. In the establishment of the superego we have before us, as it were, an example of the way in which the present is changed into the past. [*ibid.*, pp. 205–207]

Notes

1. Jean-Paul Sartre's father died before he was born, cited by Lifton (1993).
2. In the classic Walt Disney film *Pinocchio* (1944), a puppet is turned into a real, live little boy. He, Pinocchio, is advised to follow his conscience.
3. In his account of dream distortion and censorship, Freud compares the dreamer to the political writer.
4. These interactions may be products of fantasy.
5. Freud uses "object" in this context ambiguously in that it refers both to the other person and/or to a passion.
6. Freud first used the term in 1922 at the Berlin Psychoanalytic Congress. However, in *The Ego and the Id*, he continues to use the terms "ego ideal" and "superego" synonymously.
7. She later returned to treatment and reported further significant shifts in her life.

CHAPTER THREE

The formation and development of the system

"The fiercest morality is that of early infancy, and this persists as a streak in human nature that can be discerned throughout an individual's life. Immorality for the infant is to comply at the expense of a personal way of life. For instance a child of any age may feel that to eat is wrong, even to the extent of dying for the principle"

(Winnicott, 1963, p. 102)

"... there was the plain hand of Providence slapping me in the face and letting me know my wickedness was being watched ... whilst I was stealing a poor old woman's nigger that hadn't ever done me no harm and now was showing there's One that's always on the lookout, and ain't going to allow no such miserable doings to go only just so fur and no further, I most dropped in my tracks I was so scared"

(Mark Twain, 1884, *Adventures of Huckleberry Finn*, p. 370)

I n this chapter I discuss how the system superego originates and how it establishes itself in childhood, and subsequently how each person comes to achieve, or fails to achieve, the mature functioning of this system in adulthood. In considering these issues, it should be borne in mind that the development and transformation in question is a lifelong and complex process and, like all development, it is subject to regressive and progressive shifts, according to individual variations of both an internal and external nature.[1]

The growth of the system superego within the individual is a personal achievement that involves the adaptation of instinctual life (i.e., at the psychological level, we might speak of desires) to the life of the society in which he/she is raised. This has been described as a process in which "one phase of development leads, under the dual influence of instinctual and environmental forces, to the next stage of the *moral function*. On this viewing, the moral function may be regarded as the highest development of biological evolution . . ." (King, 2003, p. 319).[2]

The first three to six months, orality, primary narcissism, and primitive guilt

The earliest stages of the infant's life is a period when the mothering function is dominant and the infant is absolutely dependent upon it. (At this time, they together form a psychical unity, which Winnicott refers to as the "mother–infant unit".) At this stage, the maternal (i.e., auxiliary) ego is engaged in structuring the primitive elements of the infant ego, which normally will gradually gain cohesion, strength, power, and stability. It is the "ordinary" mother's capacity to love, protect, and be reliable, consistent, and able to establish limits that are crucial for the infant's future journey towards the development of mental health, in a general sense, and in relation to the system superego.

This developmental phase, of "absolute dependence" is one in which the infant has developed primitive and fragmented "ego-nuclei", but not yet a coherent "ego-self" (Glover, 1932; Winnicott, 1962). It is a time of "unintegration" (see Abram, 1996; Winnicott, 1945), when the maternal function contributes significantly to the nature and quality of the infant's "introject" (i.e., an imagined, internal mental structure which is a representation of the object inside). The formation of this introject anticipates and facilitates the later development of the superego system, and this will eventually enable the infant to establish a greater autonomy.[3]

At this very early period, the instinctual drives are in the ascendancy and, at first, they are thought to appear external to the infant. In healthy development, the ego gradually achieves mastery over the id impulses, in that the bodily satisfactions facilitate the strengthening of the ego itself. However, these small, gradual achievements are relatively unstable and tend to be gained then lost.

In describing the very earliest stage of infantile sexuality, Freud (1905e) referred to a period of "auto-eroticism" in which the infant obtained satisfaction from the body, without recourse to an object. He stated that "the autoerotic instincts are there from the first". However, from a theoretical standpoint, he often conflated these tendencies with the state of *primary narcissism*.[4]

Primary narcissism is a state of mind in which the primitive self unconsciously takes itself as a part-object, and in which it invests psychic energy (for example, as when the infant sucks his thumb). The gratification arising from such activity may be described as "blissful", in the sense that the infant dwells entirely in a fantasy world which temporarily excludes the normal frustrations of outer reality. Freud considered that this left a memory trace of "boundless self-sufficiency". He described this state of mind as involving the child's belief in a grandiose self-omnipotence of thought and feeling ("the centre and core of creation as we once fancied ourselves"). This gave rise to his famous phrase, "His Majesty The Baby" (Freud, 1914c, p. 91).[5]

From the viewpoint of the developing superego system, Freud considered that the ego ideal originated as a narcissistic formation and one that in later development was never wholly given up.[6]

At this earliest stage of life, mother and baby are merged in fantasy, and the infant's primitive state of mind has been variously described as "a blooming, buzzing confusion" (William James), as "unintegrated ... unpatterned and unplanned" (Winnicott, 1988) and also as an "unpatterned, interpenetrative mix" (Balint, 1968, see also Barnett, 2001). On the other hand, Klein, as will be summarized below, describes the mental life of the infant as dominated by aggressive fantasies and the anxious reaction to them.

In contrast, Winnicott's focus is less on the infant's innate, unconscious phantasies and more on the mother–infant interaction in the "holding phase". He describes the unintegrated ego (i.e., "the ego nuclei") as becoming more structured and unified so that the infant gradually moves towards the achievement of "unit status" (i.e., the state of being a person). This growth process includes the beginning of a differentiation between "me" and "not me", an appreciation of an "inside" and of an "outside", and a growing capacity for object relationships. Such development occurs in parallel with the gradual separation from the mother and a beginning of relating to her objectively as "not me". It also marks the beginning of what will be a significant development in the ego/superego system, i.e., "the capacity for concern".[7]

The infant's experience at the hands of the actual caretaker is a mixture of gratification (e.g., recognition of the mother's face) and frustration (e.g., loss of the nurturing breast). He/she grows mentally via a continuous series of subtle conscious and unconscious, verbal and non-verbal, back and forth interactions with the caretaker. In this way, the object world is built up and internalized and the infant gradually separates and evolves a "self" (Jacobson, 1964).

As development proceeds, this self becomes differentiated from a "non-self", and attains an increasingly coherent and stable existence. This individualized personhood, which in the parents' perception has been present from the beginning, is now achieved by the child when it is able to differentiate itself from the mother (i.e., in the sense of *I am!* and *You are*). These basic features of ego development are essential prerequisites for a superego system to come into existence (i.e., the origin of *You ought!*).[8]

In her original and seminal theoretical contributions, Melanie Klein has drawn attention to the presence of features in the infant's early life that contribute significantly to a superego system (e.g., early oedipal fantasies). Drawing on her experience of analysing very young children, she stresses the significance of the infant's aggression from the beginning of life, and she suggests that the infant has innate unconscious knowledge. According to Klein, this gives rise to complex, primitive, guilt-ridden fantasies. These are not only present in the infant's mind from birth, but continue to play a decisive role in all development. In her view, a complicated interplay of projective and introjective processes are operative from birth.

She describes "the paranoid–schizoid position", in which the infant is said to deal with his innate loving and destructive impulses by splitting both his ego and his object into "good" and "bad" parts (e.g., "mother's breast", "father's penis"). The destructive impulses are projected on to the object which is then perceived as "bad", and by whom the infant now feels persecuted. According to Klein, this is the infant's first attempt to master the death instinct, which from the outset is directed against the self. When the persecuting bad object is reintrojected by the infant, *the early core of the superego is formed.*

Between the ages of three months and two years, the infant, "in health", gradually reaches "the depressive position", when the part-object of the earlier phase has become a whole object (Klein, 1935, 1940). She regarded this stage as marking an early development of the child's superego system (Hinshelwood, 1989; Klein, 1940).

At this time, the infant has become sensitive to both its love and its hate being directed towards the *same* person. When the depressive position has been achieved, the infant also becomes capable of feeling sadness, primitive guilt, and primitive remorse, and these feelings are the earliest precursors of the superego system. Accompanying the achievement of the depressive position are the infant's significant defences against it (i.e., the manic defence and the various processes of reparation) and these processes are sometimes summed up in the term "depressive superego".[9]

An assumption of importance in this theory is that, in order to resolve the innately driven conflict and fantasy formations, the infant must successfully introject a stable, and predominantly "good", whole object. This assumption is consistent with Winnicott's emphasis on the significance of the holding, caring, and communicative capacities of the (actual) "environment mother", i.e., the maternal provision at the earliest stages of development.

Six to twelve months: the infant and the growth of socialized morality

In early childhood, the parents, or those who care for the infant, sooner or later seek to condition its behaviour by means of a conduct system of "do's and don'ts". The effect of this regime of rewards and prohibitions will be registered in the child's internal world, and will gradually grow to become a set of standards, which then connect to the *primitive ego ideal*. For example, a child of nine months who is responsive to its mother's commands will begin to move in the direction of obtaining its own self-command system. As growth proceeds, the parents seek to help the child gain some autonomy over its impulse life by using disciplinary methods. In this way, the child begins to internalize a *primitive morality system*, which will include images of the parents, and which will gradually become part of the self (Rayner, 1978, p. 67).[10]

That which is internalized in this way, and temporarily held, is not simply a perception of the actual caretaker, but an image likely to be influenced by such qualities as the child's projections and immature perceptions, the strength of his/her drives, the quality and nature of the fantasy life, and the level of frustration tolerance. The child's reaction to the caretaker's commands is thus a highly individualized matter.

When things do not go well and tension and distress are predominant, the introject may become distorted and develop a primitive, harsh, and cruel quality, and this may become the foundation of the superego system.

In interaction with the early fantasied *ego ideal*, the infant continues to develop a wishful image of *an ideal self*. This self is based on the earliest real (and imagined) loving and gratifying features of the relationship with the mothering figure. Furthermore, the infant contributes its own grandiose wishes to the quality of the relationship, so as to increase the pleasurable experience.

The child perceives the caretaker as omnipotent and perfect, which provides the basis for the internal formation of *an ideal object*. An important shift has occurred in the development of the superego system when the task of gaining the ideal object's love becomes of greater significance than the gratification of the child's drives.

28/5
5.45

Twelve months to two years: the socialization of the "toddler"

In the second year of life, the increased mobility and the development of language and numerous other skills mark the movement from infant to "toddler" status. The toddler, if thriving in a good-enough developmental situation (i.e., one in which there are predominantly loving and controlling caring relationships), gradually comes to internalize the rules and standards that have been trans-mitted by the parents. At this time, the toddler's wish to express its will is usually opposed by the caretakers' command to control its impulse life, and this situation leads to external and internal conflict. The toddler will tend to check on the mothering figure's emotional signals, either before or after a prohibited act, as if seek-ing confirmation about the pattern of behaviour being perceived as "right" or "wrong".

In this way, the child learns that the love it receives is increas-ingly conditional and relates to an idea of "an ideal child" in the mother's (and father's) mind (see Freud, 1912/1913, where Freud associates the child's primary narcissism with that of the parents).

When the toddler is left to struggle with the wish to express itself and the opposing wish to please its mother and to conform to her ideal, a situation develops which maximizes its ambivalence. The resolution of this problem is facilitated by the toddler's wish for the approval of *the ideal parent*, which reinforces its approval of the self (i.e., the development of "self-esteem"). This development is another necessary step and precursor towards the later achieve-ment of the more mature superego.

This third phase in the child's life is also one that centres on anal concerns. The parental attempts to control and socialize the child's impulse is exemplified in the demand that the child restrict bowel movements to a time and place of their choosing. A code of behav-iour is thus communicated to the child in subtle ways and the term "sphincter morality", coined by Sandor Ferenczi (1924, p. 267), has been used to describe the caretaker's commands and the toddler's normal compliance with this code. Such compliance will tend to modify the child's behaviour, strengthen the process of internal control and, in time, lead to an identification with the parental standards.[11]

However, if the child's view of the parents as ideal becomes spoiled and the child feels generally unsupported and threatened by the loss of their love, it may come to overvalue what it experi-ences as harsh and punishing demands and respond to them with over-idealization and over-compliance.[12]

This, when reinforced by the child's anger, may lead to the devel-opment of "perfectionist and critical introjects", which, when turned aggressively against the self, may result in its adopting a behaviour pattern of passive surrender and hostile dependence. In the extreme case, a chronic, repetitive, masochistic pattern of over-compliance and loss of spontaneity may become a permanent part of the character (Freud, 1914c, p. 101, where he describes the ego ideal in detail and links it with neurosis; see also Tyson and Tyson, 1990).

At the stage when only the rudiments of internalized self-control have been established, the external caretaker's input remains a dominant source of influence (Winnicott, 1960a, p. 42).

However, the child's gradual attainment of more stable and cohesive introjects (which are unconsciously experienced as sources of authority) will eventually lead to the establishment of more stable internal controls. However, for such interpersonal dynamics to become an *intrapsychic superego system* involves a twofold process. The first developmental step is the internalization of the parental moral codes and controls, and the second (much stressed by Freud) is the identification with these values.

Development between two and three years: "guilt" and other superego precursors

Between the ages of two and three years, there is a significant advance in the child's cognitive and affective growth and this facilitates its capacity for conformity and self-control. By the age of three, the child can potentially respond to its introject (i.e., he/she can potentially act in a self-controlled way in accordance with the demands of "the other", e.g., the mother's wishes when she is not present).

Around the age of two, it has been observed that a child who is aware of the effect of self on others may express a wish to be "good" to please its mother. For example, "Mummy, John will be a good boy today". With further internalization, say at around three, such a wish may become more directly centred in the ego/self, e.g., "I'll try to be good today". Wishes of this kind, when unsuccessful, may also produce self-accusation, guilt, and remorse.

However, at this time, issues that relate to body management remain a focus for conflict between parent and child. The child's efforts to resolve such conflict are assisted by reaction formations, and it is these which facilitate a "self-critical capacity".[13]

The loss of self-love and feelings of shame are linked to the failure to control impulse (as in soiling behaviour). The presence of these affects indicates a further development of the precursors of the superego system. The child's gradual establishment of a loving maternal introject and a loveable "self-image" imply a healthy development of the system.[14]

However, it should be understood that, in actuality, the whole developmental situation in the first three years of life remains relatively unstable and uneven, i.e., progressive and sometimes regressive. The toddler's demonstrations of remorse and shame are, therefore, not necessarily reliable signs that it has adequate control over its impulses and behaviour. Since the situation is relatively unstable, it follows that, although guilt feelings may be present in the child's mind, they may not be effective in preventing "bad" behaviour.[15, 16]

Manifestations of guilt in these early years could be regarded as "premoral", in that, as has been emphasized above, the child at this developmental stage does not yet have a superego structure that is stable and can be recognized as his own. However, with time and increasing maturity, the child will begin to develop expectations of punishment. At first, however, these are felt as coming from the parent rather than originating in the self, since the child does not yet have a stable system of guilt-induced self-punishment, i.e., conscience. Mobility has an important effect on superego development. For example, in his crawling and walking activities, the toddler becomes quickly aware of how he can create pleasure and distress in his parents. In this way, the child begins to develop an early capacity for concern about the real or fantasied damage he is capable of causing to others or to the environment (Rayner, 1978, p. 67).

Three to six years: the period of oedipal development

Following Freud's original formulations, the oedipal process and oedipal constellation have been described by a number of psychoanalytic writers (e.g., Laplanche & Pontalis, 1973, pp. 282–287).

The following is a summary of this development in the child between three and five years.[17]

Freud's view of early sexual development is that both boys and girls gradually develop an "infantile genital organisation" (each having similar sexual fantasies) in the years from birth to approximately the age of three years. Beyond this age, the child proceeds towards an "oedipal stage", in which a pattern of cross-identifications with the parents becomes an important feature of development (i.e., the oedipal triad).

One such identification is with the same sex parent, who is idealized, and it is this process that plays a further significant role in superego formation (Tyson & Tyson, 1990, p. 215).

The identifications with both parents stimulate unconscious phantasies, and these, which involve both love and hate, contribute to more and more complex inner conflicts. Thus, a move towards one parental figure may be experienced as a painful move away from the other. Also superimposed on this situation are residual conflicts from earlier developmental stages, and these conscious and unconscious memories further complicate the child's tumultuous inner phantasy life. With increasing internalization, these conflicts will become part of the superego system itself (i.e., they become self-driven).

Some time between birth and three years, the child (at least in unconscious phantasy) perceives the parents as different (for example, the father is seen as physically stronger) and also similar (both parents seem like giants, and perhaps gods). In relation to the body, both boys and girls gain some conscious awareness of their gender by about two years, and will identify themselves with the same sex parent. Such sexual awareness will include the child's own genitals. As development proceeds, the genital area takes on increasing importance and becomes a focus for physical arousal with an accompanying unconscious phantasy. The latter is reinforced by the parents' own phantasies and taboos. The pattern of inner (private) and unconscious sexual fantasy is referred to as the Oedipus complex. The theory implies that every child has a uniquely patterned constellation of fantasies and feelings, which are centred on a triangular structure involving the parents and also siblings when present.

Between the ages of three and five years, the child seeks to negotiate and master the Oedipus complex and, according to psychoanalytic theory, this experience has a central role generally in building the personality, and more specifically in the formation of the superego system.[18]

In classical theory, the superego (at least in the case of the little boy) is formed as a result of the identifications made with the father in order to avoid castration (i.e., the feared consequence of such bodily damage) and to resolve Oedipal conflict. The internalization of the system superego requires the resolution of the Oedipus complex.[19]

The child's fears of harm to the body and the loss of parental love, therefore, act to facilitate the formation of the superego system. In addition, the idealization of the parents leads the child to admire and accept the parental codes of conduct, and thence eventually to model a personal morality on their example. With continuing development, the child's fear of the loss of parental love is replaced by the loss of love of his own superego. The superego's disapproval results in self-punishment and this may be experienced as loss of self-esteem, or as a sense of guilt ("superego guilt"). As this developmental process continues, there occurs a further identification with the superego's ideals and demands, which paradoxically increases the child's internal resources, including self-esteem. As guilt comes to serve a signal function ("signal guilt"), the child becomes more sensitive in avoiding those situations that may arouse intense guilt, and behaviour becomes more attuned to the internalized moral values.

In this way, the earlier introjects and ideals are reorganized and reintegrated and the superego system becomes more coherent. However, a diminishing of the "self" (i.e., a narcissistic injury) may arise from the impossibility of gratifying the hidden wishes and the threat from a more powerful and hostile oedipal rival, but this again paradoxically contributes to the strengthening of the internalization. In other words, the more that the oedipal conflicts are taken inside by the child, the greater the threat becomes of losing the superego's love. With increasing internalization and structure, the superego acts so as to increase the sources of self-punishment. These will include guilt feelings, loss of self-esteem, and a sense of inferiority. To cope with this situation, the child becomes responsive to the demands and standards of "the ideal" that the superego system has embodied. Gradually, as the identifications in the inner world become more consistent, conflicts are lessened and self-esteem is increased. However, although the system becomes increasingly internalized and coherent at this stage of development, its dynamics tend to remain unstable and inconsistent.

The painful affect of *oedipal guilt* is very significant in this development. As this affect grows and comes to serve a signal function (cf. Freud's *moral anxiety*), the child comes habitually to behave according to its own fledgling internal moral standards, which now include a self-punitive agent. In this way, the forbidden oedipal wishes are slowly given up. However, since the inner controls stay weak and the drive impulses remain strong, the child may behave inconsistently. In fact, as Freud emphasized, the individual, throughout life, becomes increasingly aware of the *voice of conscience* and inner feelings of guilt. However, it should be noted that the actual functioning of the superego system, even in adulthood, is never totally stable, reliable, or predictable.

How crucial the child's resolution of the Oedipus complex is to the formation of the superego, however, is not entirely clear. Some children still struggle with the complex, for example, although they may already have achieved an autonomous system (Holder, 1982).

These Oedipal wishes may result in feelings of guilt, because, as has already been described, the superego makes no distinction between the wish and the action (Freud, 1930a, p. 128).

Important factors in establishing a functional superego system are "internal modifications through defense and compromise" (Tyson & Tyson, 1990, p. 220). Thus, the child achieves increased responsibility for its behaviour by identifying with its own internal standards (Rayner, 1978, p. 93).

However, when the child cannot relinquish its quest for oedipal gratifications, the formation and functioning of its superego system will be affected, leading to a consequent lack of autonomy. This is evidenced by rapid changes in the child's self-esteem, a lack of consistent behaviour, and over-reliance on "the other" for the control of impulsive behaviour.

The discussion so far has ignored gender differences in the course of oedipal development, and these will now be considered in some detail.

Male oedipal development

From birth, the little boy typically learns to love and hate his mother. At the same time, both mother and son become aware of the physical difference between them, and the boy's penis becomes a focus by which means love and hate can be expressed in fantasy.

The boy's father is also loved and hated, but he is experienced differently to the mother because he is like the boy himself. However, the father is also different in certain ways, in that, for example, he has a much bigger body and penis, and these perceptions influence the boy to regard his father as a sexual rival in the love competition for the mother. This situation is termed oedipal (or phallic) rivalry. The boy also experiences, and is sensitive to, being shut out of the intimate relationship between his parents, which is symbolized by the bedroom (and the parental intercourse or primal scene). All these experiences reinforce the reality for the boy that the mother is not his sole possession. With further physical growth, his experience of sexual excitement in relation to his penis is increased, and, in his fantasy, any damage to it may be perceived as a punishment for his oedipal wishes (i.e., on the basis of "an eye for an eye").

Both parents set standards and values for the boy in the early phases of superego development but, at the Oedipal stage, the ensuing conflicts are reorganized. Although the mother may be seen as controlling and omnipotent, the boy becomes aware that he has something not possessed by the mother, and this modifies the feelings of helplessness and anger attached to the conflicts. He increasingly gains a cumulative sense of "maleness" that links him with the authority of his idealized father. This tendency to identify with his father is very important for the boy's further development.

As the paternal introject is strengthened, the maternal demands and prohibitions become "reorganised, transformed, and directed towards the father". This process, at least in part, acts to free the boy from the early established hateful feelings towards the mother, and these are thus reduced. However, because of the boy's oedipal failure, ambivalence towards the father remains a significant challenge to the boy's development and, if this problem is unresolved, it may result in his devaluing the father and his experience of "maleness". On the other hand, a successful resolution will lead to further idealization, and identification with the "father-ideal" and acceptance of "the father's 'law' ". It follows that the challenging conflicts involved, and their further resolution, act to strengthen the superego system. It has also been observed that, since boys begin superego formation later than girls, their *archaic superego* features are likely to be less primitive and may, therefore, be easier to modify at a later stage (Tyson & Tyson, 1990, pp. 241–245).

Female oedipal development

Oedipal development and superego formation in the girl proceeds along rather different lines. For a number of reasons, this development is relatively more complicated, and more controversial, than the situation of the boy. In the case of the little girl, it seems likely that, since the genital is physically inside her, she comes to perceive (consciously and unconsciously) her father's body as physically different from her own. Evidence gathered by child psychotherapists suggests, however, that she desires to love and hate her father with her whole body and, in order to do so (in phantasy), she unconsciously wishes him to be physically inside her (*ibid.*, p. 90).

The girl, however, also loves and hates her mother, and physically identifies with her, though, at the same time, she perceives herself as much smaller. This latter perception is also reinforced by her awareness of her parents' sexual intimacy. The parents' close relationship also strengthens the girl's rivalry and envy (an affect which is considered by both Freud and Klein to be central to development). The girl sees the mother as smaller and weaker than the father, a perception that arouses her anger and contempt for her mother, whom she blames for not making her a little boy (i.e., who will grow up to become like Daddy).

All these unconscious phantasies are heightened at around the age of three, when the little girl becomes fully aware that she has a "lack" (i.e., a penis, in the sense of "something that sticks out"). Henceforth, according to Freud, she unconsciously (and therefore, involuntarily) comes to envy all males as a result of this perception of a lack or an absence.

As was noted in Chapter Two, Freud, on the basis of these differences, concluded that the little girl's superego system is weak and unstable, because she cannot experience similar castration anxiety and identification, with the father, as is the case with the boy. However, she does fear bodily damage by the mother as a result of her loving wishes towards, and competitive desire for, the father.

According to Freud, the anatomical difference between the sexes has, therefore, significant consequences for superego development in adulthood. In a famous (infamous?) passage he comments:

> For women the level of what is ethically normal is different from what it is in men. Their super ego is never so inexorable, so impersonal, so independent of its emotional origins as we require it to be in men . . . they show less sense of justice than men . . . they are less ready to submit to the great exigencies of life . . . they are more often influenced in their judgements by feelings of affection or hostility—all these would be amply accounted for by the modification in the formation of their superego. [Freud, 1925j, pp. 257–258]

For alternative views on the origin and nature of superego development in women, see Horney (1926), Jones (1927), Klein (1928, 1929, 1930, 1933), Muller-Braunschweig (1926), Sachs (1929), Jacobson (1937, 1964), Reich (1953), Greenacre (1952), Chasseguet-Smirgel (1970), Muslin (1972), Schafer (1974), Blum (1976), Bernstein (1983), Lewis (1987), Miller (1988), and especially Tyson and Tyson (1990) for a comprehensive review.

A summary of the main objections to Freud's statement, and alternative viewpoints, are now discussed below.

It is suggested that Freud's views are biased to the extent that they are based on a male model (i.e., they are phallocentric). There is also much evidence that women suffer conscious and unconscious guilt as much as men. A woman's major fears are centred on her primary object, the mother, whom she perceives as grandiose, omnipotent, and castrating. However, she also fears loss of love from, separation from, and abandonment by, the mother. She envies the mother's possession of the father and, via projection and introjection, feels herself to be envied by her.

It seems likely that a *primitive superego system* (an archaic superego) is developed by the girl to cope with such fears in the first six to twelve months of life, and its source lies in early identifications with part-objects. The archaic superego is typically experienced in extremes of "good" and "bad". In fantasy, fears of bodily damage by the mother may force the girl to give up her oedipal wishes, and these are overtaken by the girl's desire to be male. The powerful mother threatens, "*You must not have your own law!*". The little girl's guilt arises from her wishes to possess the father's penis inside her, and from her murderous feelings towards the rivalrous mother. However, she may adapt to this dilemma by remaining a "subservient" child.

From an early age, the involvement of the little girl with the father is also intense. This may involve a "primary, passive, masochistic wish to be violated by the fantasized penis" ("father", "maleness"), and this image is idealized and contributes to *a core superego*. In girls, "deprivation anxiety" is as intense as castration anxiety. The girl's fears are transferred to the father in the oedipal phase. *Superego anxiety* is based on the ideal of renunciation, in that the girl has to abandon oedipal wishes and tolerate the resulting frustration. Unconsciously, she desires her father and wishes to have his baby, and her (again unconscious) resolution is either to become fixated on the father or to accept "deprivation as a life-long ideal".

The superego system evolves differently in girls and women, because the absence of a penis is experienced as a narcissistic injury and, as has already been suggested, the mother may be blamed for this, and she (and the female genital) devalued. One form of adaptation to this situation is to form *an ideal* of becoming neat, clean, and obedient. There is a developmental shift of focus in the girl from the genital to the whole body, and from the mother to the father; she may become anxious with regard to the father's love (represented by the penis) and this concern would then return her to the early notion of injury through absence. To attempt a resolution, the girl may invest in her father's moral ideas and values, and thus "the female anxiety of conscience becomes a secondary social anxiety". The girl's attitude towards her own femininity also depends on the parents' affirmation, though without exploitation of it. The achievement of a mature ego ideal and an autonomous superego in a woman depend on her acceptance of her femininity, and on her refinding the previously abandoned maternal identifications.

There is much evidence (e.g., self-attacking behaviour) to suggest that the system superego in women is not so much "inferior" and "weak", as Freud had originally suggested, but rather follows a more "complicated pathway" of functioning and development. An important gender difference relates to the contents of prohibitions and moral codes. In relation to women in society, there is much greater focus on sexual and aggressive activity, and such familiar ideals as the expectation of "sweetness" in personality, and the demands and constraints of becoming a future mother. The superego system in women, compared with men, appears to favour flexibility above firmness, and the dictates of human relationship rather than abstract law (Tyson & Tyson, 1990, p. 235).

In summary, the female person's conflict with the same sex parent must be resolved in favour of positive feelings, before the system can continue to develop. The central feature in development appears to be the powerful tie to the mother, and the problem for the girl of moving beyond it. If an intense hatred of the mother persists, it will tend to set up a harsh, critical, and punitive superego.[20]

In resolving the dilemmas, the role of the father is also crucial, since he is in a position to rescue the girl from her conscious and unconscious entanglements with the mother. His use of his authority, power, and care can make him into an alternative love object, and help in mediating the hostility felt towards the mother. It follows that the quality of the relationship between father and daughter may significantly affect the nature of, and adjustments to, her system superego.

A literary example

As an illustration of the problems of superego development in a young woman, I once more return to George Eliot's portrayal of her heroine, Gwendolen, in *Daniel Deronda* (see Note 13, Chapter One). This portrait is particularly relevant, since it not only provides a valuable picture of female development, but also illustrates the growth of a superego system and a sense of personal morality (see Chapters One and Two).[21]

Gwendolen is in her early twenties and has many qualities. Among these are her beauty, charm, intelligence, vitality, and her witty playfulness. However, she is also described as ignorant, wilful, and powerful, in that she dominates the mother and her half-siblings. She is also "rootless" and her air of "crude self-confidence" hides a general immaturity. Added to a narrowness of outlook, are an insistent demand for gratification of her wishes, a tendency to over-estimate her powers, and a dominant egotism. She is portrayed as living almost entirely for "self" and, throughout the novel, is largely unable to empathize with others who are living their separate centres of consciousness.

Most significant of all with regard to personality, however, are a number of hysterical traits described as definite yet vague, e.g., "fits of spiritual dread", which on occasion give rise to bouts of hysterical screaming ("a brief remembered madness", see Chapter Two). The episodes in which this behaviour is displayed make her vexed, since they fall far short of a conscious "ideal" that she has set herself. This is: "being daring in speech . . . reckless in braving dangers, both moral and physical". As I have previously described, she shows other neurotic elements, which include fears of being alone, being loved, certain changes in the light, and agoraphobia.

How these "terrors" are connected with Gwendolen's background becomes clearer as the action of the novel unfolds. For example, we are told of her biological father's death when she is aged twelve ("Dear papa had died when his little daughter was in long clothes."). She has also experienced a failed relationship with her "unlovable", and much absent, stepfather (a Captain Davilow), who is also deceased. In combination with her beauty and other influences, these circumstances lead her to have problems with her mother and, more generally, with men.

The portrait of Mrs Davilow, the mother, is of a child-like personality with weak and depressive features. She loves, but is also over-indulgent towards, Gwendolen, who is spoiled and is presented as a "princess in exile". The relationship also suffers from a mutual over-dependence and is subject, at times, to a significant role reversal.[22]

The mother's second unsatisfactory remarriage to a frequently absent, and neglectful, naval officer has nevertheless resulted in the birth of four half-sisters. This situation leads Gwendolen to perceive her family as one in which her stepfather had possessed and stolen her mother. This causes Gwendolen to have a resentful attitude towards the mother, to envy the stepfather and, especially, to exhibit unconscious murderous behaviour towards her half-sisters.

Nevertheless, when the family is threatened by poverty, Gwendolen responds by agreeing to a "marriage of convenience", and this decision has fateful consequences for her life, and specifically for her moral development, to which I now turn.

Eliot's Gwendolen has been described as a "neurotic, selfish, suffering but superbly integrated character who is one of the greatest psychological studies in English fiction".[23]

In what follows, this observation should be borne in mind, since my description, which focuses only on her development of a personal morality, is necessarily reductionist and schematic and cannot, therefore, do justice to Eliot's full portrayal of a complex young woman in late adolescence and early adulthood.

A significant image in the novel is of a painting that is situated in a wall panel usually kept closed, but which is opened by accident to reveal an "upturned *dead* face from which an obscure figure seems to be fleeing with outstretched arms". The sight of this image ignites a latent dread in Gwendolen, which stimulates and connects together a fear of murderous impulse and a dread of conscience ("the region of guilt, which forbids impulse"), described as "something within her which troubled satisfaction" (Eliot, 1876, p. 362).

As I have previously indicated, the decision to marry Grandcourt is one based on expediency and represents a failure of conscience in the sense of an act of wrongdoing that is feared. Gwendolen has previously promised Grandcourt's former mistress, Lydia Glasher (with whom Grandcourt has fathered two children), that she will not agree to this proposal of marriage and thereby will leave the way open for Mrs Glasher. On her wedding night, she receives a letter from Mrs Glasher, which causes an outburst of hysterical screaming in Gwendolen, and "an accusing apparition" continues to haunt her throughout the novel.[24]

Both parties experience the marriage as a struggle and quest for power and dominance. Gwendolen loses this battle and becomes desperately unhappy, since she is increasingly tortured by a pattern of dread and misery that has many strands. She is humiliated by "the sin of deception", in that she feels that the knowledge of the meeting with Mrs Glasher must be kept secret from Grandcourt. She is also frightened by her thoughts of a "desperate rebellion" against her cruel, taunting, and dominating husband. Another aspect of her dread is the possibility of becoming a mother, which would further complicate her "wrong-doing" towards Mrs Glasher. Most powerful of all, however, are the intrusive thoughts that her hope of escape from the marriage lay in her husband's death. These thoughts had added to the dread of her husband, the dread of "self", and especially the dread of her (near-conscious) murderous wishes towards him.[25, 26] 2.00

2.55

I turn now to Daniel's "fatherly" role in the growth of Gwendolen's conscience. At the opening of the novel, he observes Gwendolen in an impulse-driven gambling activity, and one of which he strongly disapproves. However, she also fascinates him, since he sees in her a "self" that is representative of everything "good" and "bad" that he is not. In fact, she remains under his moral "gaze" from the beginning to the end of the novel, in that he acts towards her as a corrective presence, and it is this that is gradually internalized by her.

Eliot writes that Daniel comes to take hold of her mind as "one who had an unknown standard by which he judged her".[27]

As I have described above, the past influences on her have been largely determined by her mother's "timid maternal conscience" and the absence of her father in her upbringing. Throughout the novel, she becomes increasingly able to see herself through Daniel's eyes, and he becomes a force which offers her the "hope" that she will be able to fight her dread of wrongdoing and "hidden helplessness".[28]

As Gwendolen's unhappiness deepens, the previously vague "dread" begins to take shape, in that she will commit "some fiercely impulsive deed" that will lead not to release, but to an accumulation of new guilt and terrors ("a white dead face from which she was for ever trying to flee and for ever held back").

The plot takes a significant turn when Grandcourt, in spite of bad weather warnings, persuades her to accompany him on a yachting trip. At this time, Gwendolen's mind is on her quite conscious murderous "internal" wishes:

> . . . her own wishes, which were taking shapes possible and impossible, like a cloud of demon-faces. She was afraid of her own hatred, which under the cold iron touch that had compelled her today had gathered a fierce intensity . . . quick, quick came images, plans of evil . . . like furies preparing the deed that they would straightway avenge. [p. 753]

When Grandcourt is drowned and Gwendolen has been rescued, she is met and "counselled" by Daniel, to whom she relates the details of what has happened.[29]

Her mental state is now such that she cannot distinguish between what she has done and what she has not, between the murderous thoughts and an actual act of killing her husband.[30] Daniel, however, considers her obvious remorse "the precious sign of a recoverable nature ... awakening a new life within her" and her recovery now depends totally on Daniel, who offers the following advice: "... the burden on your conscience is what no one ought to be admitted to the knowledge of ... let your remorse tell only on the use that you will make of your monetary independence" (p. 850).[31]

As the novel draws to a close, Gwendolen identifies Daniel with "the struggling regenerative process within her". She experiences this as a process that demands "acceptance of rebuke—the hard task of self change—confession—endurance". But, and it is a large qualification, she remains in a state of "unconscious reliance and expectation", and therefore, in an extreme and precarious state of dependence.[32]

However, in spite of this, Gwendolen gradually grows calmer. She is helped in this change by Daniel's advice (i.e., he suggests that she lessens the "demands for self" and that she accepts "the ordinary good of existence"). A growing inner strength now enables her to face the next great shock and crisis in her life, when Daniel tells her of his imminent marriage and of his planned departure to Palestine.[33]

She is profoundly distressed, and made physically ill by the shock of this news, but she is able, to some extent, with her mother in attendance, to work through this grief towards a new set of expectations: "Bursting out hysterically", she said "... 'Don't be afraid. I am going to live.' ". Her "fits of shrieking" become interspersed with signs that, in working through her grief, she has developed a new empathy and a capacity for concern. (" 'Ah poor Mamma! You have been sitting up with me. Don't be unhappy. I shall live. I shall be better.' ").[34]

However, the novel ends on an ambiguous note in relation to Gwendolen's further development. Except for her mother's presence, she stands alone, a widow facing a painful new beginning and an uncertain future. It is as if George Eliot avoids a romantic "happy ending", and rather affirms that real life is tough and uncertain.

Latency and the school-aged child: further socialization from 5–6 to 10–11 years

During the latency period, the child, in health, strives towards a reduction of dependency on the parents, and this is partly achieved through the growth and strengthening of the ego, and at the bidding of the superego. The primary school aged child develops an inner voice that represents authority, and this is less fierce and condemnatory of impulse life than its earlier version that had been dominated by more primitive introjects.

At the beginning, the five-year-old's superego system tends to rigidity, inconsistency, and externalization, since it is a distorted version of the external world. Behaviour may vary and range from the outrageous, impulse-driven kind, to "telling tales out of school". In everyday affairs, the drive pressure may win the battle over internal restraint, and this may result in "vulnerable self-esteem". However, ethical principles, rules, and fairness become established as major constraints at this time. The immersion in a new environment (i.e., the school) in fact provides a unique opportunity for the growth of the child's "conscience".[35]

In the UK, when a child has legally to begin full-time school at the age of five (but may have attended a nursery school at an earlier age), he/she has already made some adjustment to the parents' habits, values, and morality. Once the child starts school and is put in the charge of a teacher (acting *in loco parentis*), she may present the child with a different point of view to that of the parents. If this difference is substantial, it can become a significant source of conflict. At this time, the child also finds himself in the company of other children from different backgrounds and value systems. This new dimension in the child's life can, of course, have both positive and negative effects on his growth and well-being. However, whatever the outcome, the necessary adaptation to school life is a highly significant one for the continuing development of the superego system, which, as Freud noted, is always tied closely to a predominant culture.

The development of the superego is greatly helped by the teachers' efforts to encourage disciplined thought, socialized behaviour, and new skills, in children of this age. Such socialization, however, may encounter a certain resistance, because of the child's natural, and healthy, "self-willed imagination", and his/her "wild fantasy" (Rayner, 1978, p. 101). For a beautifully imagined treatment of this conflict, see Mark Twain's *Huckleberry Finn*, in which Huck prefers his individual freedom to live his own life and resists the *civilizing* attempts by the Widow Douglas ("who took him for a son"), for example, "to teach him to spell".

The new challenges presented by competition with other children may have beneficial and/or adverse effects on the child. On the one hand, they may generate the excitement, and pride of achievement, in learning new skills and gathering new friendships. The child's adjustment to the group dynamics of his peers may also lead to the enjoyment of a spirit of comradeship, and a new opportunity for experiencing sharing behaviour and developing democratic attitudes.

On the other hand, the anxiety to do better than a competitor, and the fear of being shamed, may result (via projection) in bullying, teasing, and group-induced scapegoating behaviour (see Tyson & Tyson, 1990).

Referring and paying tribute to the earlier work of Klein (1932) and Anna Freud (1927b), Winnicott considered the latency period as one of "relative calm in the instinctual world" and a "period in which the ego comes into its own so to speak". He notes that, in health, the latency child is not compelled to bow to id demands, though id drives maintain force and appear in all manner of indirect forms (Winnicott, 1958).

In his account of this stage of development, he gives considerable emphasis to the presence and strength of the child's organized defences (especially repression), and the successful fending off of instinctual demands. He also mentions the threat to ego organization of the idea of "free association" and notes that the children have achieved "a sanity and left the primary process". However, he points to dangers for the child's mental health if the latency phase persists into adulthood. He suggests that this is evidenced when ego achievement is gained but the freedom of the id has been sacrificed.

A literary example: the character of Daniel

In the account so far of the developing superego system, much emphasis has been given to the influence of parental values and standards, and to the effect on the child's development of the general cultural background. To illustrate the significance of these factors, I now consider the effect on personality and character when the child has little or no knowledge of his roots. As a fictional illustration, I return to George Eliot's portrayal of her hero, Daniel, a character who provides an example of this situation.

We are introduced to him as a handsome, intelligent young man in his twenties, who has grown up without any definite knowledge of his biological parents, his ancestry, his culture, or his race. His sole knowledge, in this respect, is that his name sounds vaguely "foreign".

From an early age, he has been cared for, reared, and formally educated under the guidance of a rich, aristocratic, and kindly guardian, Sir Hugo Mallinger, whom he calls "uncle" and with whom there is mutual affection. The guardian's aim has been to provide him with the educative process by means of which the adopted son will become a Christian English gentleman. In pursuit of this aim, Sir Hugo keeps Daniel in ignorance of his actual parents and of his foreign background. Consequently, Daniel develops a dominant fantasy (consciously derived in early adolescence and reinforced by gossip) that he is his *guardian's* illegitimate son.[36] In fact, we (and he) learn, late in the novel, that he is born of non-English, Jewish parents.

This "absence" of background knowledge, and the fantasies that accompany it, clearly have significant effects on Daniel's personality and character. Eliot's portrait of him is, in a profound sense, one of a person who is "lost", unsettled in his aims, and lacking a vocation that would give meaning, focus, and direction to what is referred to as his "neutral" (neutered?) life. As he grows up, he adjusts to this significant lack of identity with what is referred to as "an extension of sympathy" towards others. Eliot writes, "*Daniel's conscience* included sensibilities beyond the common, enlarged by his earlier habit of thinking himself imaginatively into the experience of others" (p. 564). (The meaning here is perhaps closer to the modern usage of "empathy".)

As a young adult, he has developed a generalized, idealistic frame of mind and a power of nurture, which lead him to be very caring, helpful, and even therapeutic towards other people, especially (though not exclusively) women. His actions include altruistic acts of rescue, and Eliot describes how Daniel is unconsciously identified with, and motivated by, "an unfulfilled duty to a parent".

However, this portrayal of Daniel also suggests a deficiency in the ego ideal, and he develops a kind of selflessness that is personally damaging. In making this statement, I am following the definition given by Tyson and Tyson (1990): "The ego ideal refers to a collection of specific mental representations that carry model, exemplar, or wished for *standards* or ways of being. These . . . representations [are] . . . *within the superego*" (p. 198, my italics).

Using metaphor, Eliot describes how this "lack of self" can have crippling effects on the personality development. For example, she notes that in Daniel a "sense of an entailed disadvantage—the deformed foot doubtfully hidden by the shoe, makes a restlessly active spiritual yeast . . . the inexorable sorrow . . . *had given a bias to his conscience*" (p. 168, my italics).[37]

The problem with Daniel's "plenteous, flexible", and diffuse sympathy, and habit of reflection, was that they produced in him a "neutrality" and paralysis of action, and that this, in turn, led to a longing for some event, or insight, by means of which he could escape the prison of impartiality in which he was enclosed.[38]

This *defective ego ideal* had led him, by the age of twenty-five, to live his life in "a state of suspense", and this mental stance made him peculiarly vulnerable to adopting the ideals of another person, especially when these are strong and connect with a very powerful inner desire to discover "roots". This rootless mental state has consequences which are described by Eliot in the following metaphorical way: ". . . .he might receive from Mordecai's mind the complete ideal shape from that personal duty and citizenship, which lay in his own thought like sculptured fragments certifying some beauty yearned after, but not traceable by divination" (p. 565).

Puberty and adolescence

This period of development has been described by a number of analytic writers, each of whom captures a vital aspect of the dynamic process, but the actual experience itself, which is normally subject to repression, remains elusive and, to some extent, mysterious. Adolescence as a personal experience is, perhaps, better imagined and described by poets, such as Shakespeare, and other writers and artists. However, the quotations from the four analytic sources that follow are valuable attempts to define adolescence as a *process*.

> The psychological changes consequent upon puberty . . . it is a process not a state . . . [It is best referred to as] *adolescing* [and is] . . . a normal crisis of life [and like any crisis] . . . is accompanied by partial disintegration of thought and feeling . . . anxiety . . . perplexity . . . impulsive action . . . and re-emergence of primitive fantasy. [Rayner, 1978, p. 104]

> . . . a complex adjustment to . . . major physical and emotional changes . . . finding a new . . . *sense of oneself-in-the-world* . . . the means by which this relationship may be achieved vary across an enormously wide range of behaviour, of different modes of defence and adaptation, from being the "conforming", "pseudo-adult", "good" boy or girl to being the "tear-away", the "drug addict", the "suicide risk", the "bad" boy or girl . . . [Waddell, 1998, p. 126]

> . . . when we are no longer children and have not yet reached adult-hood—is a time of much disturbance, change and potential for growth. The adolescent is confronted with a body that stretches, changes and grows in all directions, as does her or his mind: he is no longer who he was. [Wise, 2000, p. 7]

> It is valuable to compare adolescent ideas with those of childhood. If in the fantasy of early growth, there is contained death, then at adolesence there is contained murder. Even when growth at the period of puberty goes ahead without major crises, one may need to deal with acute problems of management because growing-up means taking the parents' place. It really does. In the unconscious fantasy, growing up is an inherently aggressive act. And the child is no longer child-size. [Winnicott, 1971, p. 144]

The advent of puberty and adolescence is a very important developmental stage for the further growth of the system superego. I will try to describe some general features of this growth, but the reader should bear in mind the highly significant differences. These are related to such factors as gender, social class, and cultural background, as well as to individual differences. Certain of these variations will be noted as the changes in the system are explored.

At this time of challenge from the external world, the young person's internal situation is very important for the task of managing "drives, objects and ideals". The bodily changes that "explode" have psychological effects, which present a considerable challenge to the personality and, in managing this situation character features such as autonomy, spontaneity, and accepting responsibility, become of increasing significance. The theoretical implications of the new psychesoma for the healthy development of the superego system can be stated quite simply and succinctly: ". . . the superego must become fully internalised and parental authority relinquished. Finally, ego functioning must predominate over superego functioning" (Tyson & Tyson, 1990, p. 223).

Crucial to the continuing development of a strong and stable system is the young person's gradual detachment from libidinal ties to the parents, their authority, and the psychic dependency on them. This task becomes one of re-examining early introjects and ideals and shouldering authority ("killing off the parents"). This involves the loss of childhood and parental love, which requires the "work of mourning". Many analytic observers have noted that this developmental task is especially difficult, since the adolescent has to come to terms with owning new personal responsibilities, while continuing to need the experience and judgement of external authority. Many have also commented on the moodiness, misery, and isolation that often accompany these complex processes of change (see, for example, Anna Freud's (1958) account of "inner object loss").

The management of such "growing pains" may also lead to the adolescent's displacement onto idealized leaders of the peer group and others, and, as Freud noted, action-orientated and sometimes maladaptive behaviour (see, for example, Shakespeare's *Romeo and Juliet* for an outstanding fictional rendering of these intergenerational and peer feuds, which, in this example, reach tragic dimensions).

Adolescence is a time when the personal re-examination of internalized values leads to their modification in relation to external reality, and this process increases the stability of the superego system. The remodelling of the early ego ideal in relation to peers, and other idealized figures, tends to differ significantly from the actual parents, and many analysts and others have drawn attention to the meaning of the familiar "battles with parents" at this period, in which external conflict may be substituted for internal conflict. The young person's expectation is that the parents should maintain standards, in order that he/she can oppose them. Since parents are human, and also much affected by their own adolescent experience, they are primed to fail in this task (for example, the adoption of extreme, possessive, over-demanding, or over-permissive parental attitudes, is likely to result in varieties of inconsistent ego and superego functioning in the offspring).

In the midst of the many psychic challenges presented by the necessary reorganization and re-integration of the superego system, the young person will, in certain respects, remain tied to the internal structures, identifications, and idealizations of the past. The sheer size and complexity of the task of negotiating the changes involved is likely to involve a considerable time period for a "good-enough" resolution to be achieved. A successful adaptation will involve the adolescent with conscious and unconscious acceptance of some adult standards, while others will be rejected as unacceptable.

A valuable concept that can be applied to this stage of development is *secondary object constancy*. This is achieved when the old, idealized, omnipotent parental images, previously internalized into the superego system, have become "humanized". For optimum development to occur, the further modification of self and object representations is required to be in line with the current reality. If gained, it will be accompanied by an increase in, and strengthening of, self-esteem (Blos, 1967).

In healthy development, as the superego system grows, it becomes less phantasy-dominated and more consistent with family values, and with the prevailing moral standards of the community:

> . . . it functions more compassionately in its guiding, judging, criticizing and punishing dimensions. As the voice of authority is again securely lodged within the mind, the superego structure optimally gains individuality, flexibility, and stability, and it becomes a mature, autonomous, coherent, and consistently functioning psychic system. [Tyson & Tyson, 1990, p. 226]

However, analysts who work with, and describe, adolescent and adult development have always emphasized the vulnerability, instability, and relativity of the system, and the likelihood of regression to the "primitive core" under exceptional circumstances.

It should be noted that, throughout the life span, the system superego is subject to the "ups and downs" of progression, fixation, and regression, which may operate in accordance with individual, family, and societal experience. This means (as Freud maintained) that a person of any age is necessarily involved in a continuous struggle of coming to terms with the ongoing conflicts among components of the mind (i.e., the ego, the id, and the superego) in relation to the external world.

As we shall see in Chapter Five, in certain circumstances, a particular person's adaptation to changes in the external world may involve the destruction of *the capacity for concern*. Such a phenomenon is clearly indicative of a grossly abnormal development of the system superego.

Intellectual development also has an important role in the process of "adolescing". The bright-enough young person is equipped to manipulate ideas, and play with abstractions and ideals. This may, however, have negative effects (e.g., a certain "omnipotence of thought"), as well as positive effects, and the former can cause havoc in reality testing in the external world.

The mixed-up and fluid state of mind of the adolescent, characterized by the questioning, challenging and opposing of parental values, unsettles the stability of the system superego that may have been previously achieved. However, the personal dilemmas that may result also have a creative effect. The healthy adolescent, whilst struggling with the process of growing up, is stimulated to search for new values and a life guided by *a personal morality*. The desire to make the world, the environment, etc., a better place to live in has in itself a strengthening effect on the internal structure and, at least in principle, on the external world.

At this period, the primitive sense of the guilt and concern for the other, which was forged at an earlier developmental stage, has, if all goes well, matured. Now, the *more mature sense of guilt* will have a positive effect on the growth of conscience, in that it helps the young person to assess her/his actions in relation to others. As Rayner (1978, p. 108) writes, ". . . conscience in its final form has been hammered out by the young person himself . . . it becomes his own and the source of his integrity of character".

Adult development

The continuing development, functioning, and variations of the system superego in early adulthood, middle age, and old age is a vast subject covering much psychoanalytic theory and the whole life span, and will not be attempted here. However, certain more pathological aspects of the ongoing, complex relationships between the superego and the self are considered in Chapter Four, and the functioning, and malfunctioning, of the system in relation to others, in Chapter Five. Comprehensive and valuable accounts of adult development can be found in Rayner (1978) and, from somewhat different standpoints, in Waddell (1998) and Tyson and Tyson, (1990).

A literary example

A valuable account of the struggles of a young man to establish an autonomous superego system in adolescence and early adulthood, can be found in James Joyce's semi-autobiographical first novel, *Portrait of the Artist as a Young Man.*

Unlike the portrait of Daniel discussed earlier, this novel is about the very powerful effect on an individual of his well-established "roots" (his family, his background, and his culture). Joyce has his hero, Stephen Dedalus, declare his ambition at the end of the novel. This has been to "forge in the smithy of my soul the uncreated conscience of my race".[39]

The portrait of Stephen is that of a young man "hammering out" a superego system, in order to find "a personalised conscience" (i.e., one that clearly belongs to him and structures his character). The story, which is told in the first person, is an account of a struggle both to form, and to consolidate, such a conscience and a private system of values, which, though much influenced by parental and cultural factors, have also clearly been individualized.

Stephen's growth from early childhood, through adolescence, to young adulthood is described in five parts. In the course of this development, he strives to escape from the stifling atmosphere of his family, and of Dublin life in general. The constraints that he experiences include his father's intrusive values, the claustrophobia of his family circle, and the political and religious (Catholic) culture of Ireland itself. His attempt to find a way out of this maze involves him in a search for hidden, forbidden knowledge, with its accompanying dangers. Stephen's "growing up" typically involves many "ups and downs", and these are described by Joyce in a series of memories and images. His responses to circumstance are tinged with internal fantasy, and always subject to external influences, and a selection of these memories is discussed below from the viewpoint of the hero's developing superego system.

The novel begins with an infantile memory in which Stephen's father is playfully telling him a bedtime story about a "moocow" meeting "a baby tuckoo". He perceives that his father's hairy face and monacle distinguish him from his mother, whom he recognizes by her nice smell and by the tunes she plays on the piano. The family circle includes "Uncle Charles" and "Dante" (auntie), his governess. At one point, a system of "Do's and Don'ts" in action can be observed, when Stephen hides after being naughty, and is urged by his mother and Dante to "apologise". This first indication of a super-ego precursor is shown by a visual image of a very threatening and frightening kind. This is uttered by Dante, who playfully rhymes "the eagles will come and pull out his eyes" (i.e., "ap–ol–og–ise").

We next meet Stephen at a Jesuit boarding school, where he has been sent at the age of six years. Here he experiences bullying by some of the boys and also cruel treatment by a master, and he is unjustly caned. Urged on by his peers, he courageously protests to the rector about the injustice.

We see him next in the family circle (which includes Mr Casey, his father's friend) in which the participants are enjoying the food, drink, fun, and banter at a Christmas dinner. The conversation takes a more serious turn, when conflicts involving the Irish Catholic Church and political issues are discussed. Dante, who argues for the Church, now stoutly defends the involvement of the priesthood in the coming election. Her opinions contrast strongly with those of Stephen's father and Mr Casey, who resent the Church's interference in politics. As the argument develops, Dante's version of the *Catholic ego ideal* is made explicit when she says: "It is a question of public morality. A priest would not be a priest if he did not tell his flock what is right and what is wrong".

The discussion then turns to the Church's attitude to the Protestant politician, Charles Stuart Parnell, and things become very heated in that Dante, in a rage, denounces Parnell as the: "Devil out of hell! We won! We crushed him to death!" The young Stephen, who has been sitting through this entire row, escapes into reverie. He notices, however, that, when the dead Parnell is recalled, his father and Mr Casey are both in tears.[40]

As the family's fortune declines, Joyce vividly describes a change in the relationship between Stephen and his father. In addition to the poverty, Stephen is embarrassed by what he experiences as his father's incoherent chattering, his heavy drinking, empty posturing, and sense of grievance.

Now increasingly disillusioned by reality, Stephen escapes into a lonely brooding and romantic literature. In his early adolescence, a girl named Emma, who teasingly stares at him, attracts him. He is timid and unresponsive, and can only write what amounts to a "phoney" poem. In adolescent fashion, he also retreats into narcissistic indulgence (i.e., he finds comfort in admiring himself in a mirror).

Stephen's physical frustrations are eased when he meets a prostitute who initiates him into sex, but, because of his Catholic childhood, with its emphasis on conformity, obedience, and the significance of "sin", he has developed a powerful and punitive superego, and his sexual experimentation causes him considerable mental discomfort. This is greatly increased when he attends a religious retreat and is subjected to lengthy and frightening hell-fire sermons in which the many horrors of the hell, which await "unrepentant sinners", are described.

In this section, Joyce describes *the Catholic conscience* in vivid metaphors. Hideous "devil and foul demons" are pictured mocking and jeering the lost souls in Hell. The concept of conscience as a powerful and punitive voice is illustrated by the use of the interrogatory style: "Why did you sin? Why did you lend an ear to the temptings of fiends? Why did you turn aside from your pious practices and good works?"[41, 42]

In response to these sermons, he experiences strong feelings of guilt, shame ("filthy thoughts" about Emma), self-distrust, and terrified remorse. However, in his fantasy life, he imagines himself innocently hand in hand with Emma, forgiven and comforted.

Terrified by the *projection of his bad conscience* in the form of threatening faces, eyes, presences, and murmuring voices, he prays for forgiveness, but he experiences a nightmare. He now goes to confession and recounts his various sins, especially his sexual exploits.

After an ensuing self-examination, he feels himself cleansed in heart and mind, and is joyfully at peace. All this is communicated to the reader in imagery that has a kind of exaggerated self-consciousness. In a quest for spiritual and moral reformation, Stephen now becomes very religious. His superego demands also lead him to follow a life of bodily purity, personal discipline, and religious righteousness, and these command regular mortifications. However, much of this "conversion" is conceived, and acted on, in a very unreal way, so that his efforts of "self-denial" become "lost" in a sea of adolescent abstraction and idealization.

Stephen is next pictured at an interview with a director of studies, at which he is asked to consider the priesthood as a vocation. He is assured that this vocation would lead him to achieve secret knowledge and power. However, after seeing a group of young men casually passing by, he senses a coldness in the religious life, which he now thinks would threaten his solitude and "freedom" to live, and to learn, in his own way.

As he gradually moves further into early manhood, Stephen begins to consider a change from the religious to the literary life. This movement seems to indicate that he has developed a more individualized superego system. He senses that the idea of becoming a creative artist would fulfil his aim of a new life of freedom and power, and this change represents a second conversion, this time to art. Later, he theorizes that art is the attempt to embody an image of beauty in sound or shape or colour, an idea stimulated by seeing a young girl bathing in the sea. However, he realizes that, to achieve such an aim, it is necessary to separate himself from his mother and her wishes (e.g., that he should retain his religious faith). He comes now to the realization that to achieve the life of the artist (symbolized by an unfolding flower) will require him to escape from the city of Dublin itself.

However, instead of leaving the city, he enters University College, Dublin, an all-Catholic institution, which he had previously anticipated would provide a path from subjugation to freedom. Here, although he finds inspiration in the richness of words, he finds himself out of sympathy with other students. He makes various friends, but he does not share their enthusiasm for Irish nationalism or for political activity. He has also, by now, lost his faith in the Church, and he experiences nationality, language, and religion as traps that imprison and prevent the flight of his "soul" (symbolized by flying birds). The quest for "unfettered freedom" (*the personal ego/superego*), he says, will be found in a refusal to serve his home (i.e., respond to the "sobs and reproaches" of his mother), his homeland, and the Church.[43]

Stephen's "growing pains" continue in that his wish and attempt to become a poet (i.e., one who can communicate with others) does not extend to real life. For example, his prolonged and intermittent interest in the girl, Emma, who is now also a student, is sustained by image and abstraction, rather than any real contact and communication. In other words, he has substituted "sex in the head" for a more direct physical and verbal expression of his love.

At the end of the novel, Stephen is pictured as a young adult, isolated from home and country, and he now decides to leave Dublin and go into exile. In a personal journal entry, he writes of the call of distant places and the predicted companionship of fellow-exiles. He prepares to set out but, before doing so, he seeks the blessing of his ancestor, Daedalus. It is clear that, in this semi-fictional illustration, the achievement of a relatively mature system superego is connected with a great deal of significant loss. It is as if Joyce is demonstrating that a kind of maturity has, therefore, only been achieved at a considerable cost to the young person.[44]

Notes

1. In much of the discussion that follows, I am indebted to Rayner (1978), Davis and Wallbridge (1981), Olsen and Koppe (1988), Tyson and Tyson (1990), King and Steiner (1991), Waddell (1998), Hurry (1998), and Edgcumbe (2000).

2. From a paper by John Rickman (1951) on the development of the moral function.

3. For the use of "introject" and a definition of "introjection", see Laplanche and Pontalis (1973), and Tyson and Tyson (1990).

4. Freud's concepts of "auto-eroticism" and "primary narcissism" have been accepted by some analysts and questioned by a number of others,

especially object-relations theorists. For a discussion of the controversy, see Laplanche and Pontalis (1973, pp. 45–47, 337–338); Rycroft (1968, pp. 10 and 94); Winnicott (1958, pp. 262–266, 1960a, p. 44); and Barnett (2001, pp. 185–186).

5. For a beautiful illustration of the state of mind called "primary narcissism", see John Fielding's "His Majesty The Baby, Hamlet again". Unpublished talk to the Squiggle Foundation, 17 February, 1990.

6. Winnicott (1959–1964), in a paper on psychoanalytic classification, describes narcissistic development as one in which "the real individual . . . is hidden and is secretly loved and cared for by 'the self within the self' " (p. 127).

7. Winnicott (1963) makes a distinction between the "object mother" (the infant's perception of the mother when he/she is in a state of excitement) and the "environment mother" (the mother when perceived by the infant in a quiet and peaceful state of mind). The combination of these two perceptions marks the development of a "capacity for concern". See also Anna Freud's description of "object constancy" (Freud, A., 1968, p. 506) and Barnett (2006).

8. The actual developmental situation is often described by analysts working in the Kleinian tradition (and some Independent analysts) as a projective–introjective process in which the child, from early infancy, "throws out" and "takes-in" aspects of the object.

9. See Zetzel (1970). She describes how the "depressive superego" can be pushed into "melancholic self-reproach".

10. Following Freud, Klein and Winnicott, Rayner has described "primitive guilt" in children under seven.

11. The significance of the toddler's aggressive impulses and its relation to early precursors of the superego, especially infantile guilt, has also been emphasized in the analytic literature.

12. The dangers of such *false morality* is perhaps the major dimension of the theory of the False Self (see Winnicott, 1960b).

13. For a useful definition of reaction formation, see Rycroft, 1968, p. 137.

14. Guilt has been distinguished from shame as follows:

> guilt seems to be felt in response to harmful or repetitive actions or phantasies of such actions. Shame by contrast is often to do with failures to do what is expected and is associated with feelings of weakness . . . feelings of weakness, helplessness and passivity associated with shame may give rise to feelings of guilt. [Mollon, 2003, p. 67]

See also Rayner (1978) and George Eliot's description of Gwendolen Harleth in *Daniel Deronda*, p. 325.

15. For a discussion of moral anxiety, see Freud (1933a, pp. 62, 78, 85, 88), and Tyson and Tyson (1990, p. 214).

16. Anna Freud (1936) has related "identification with the aggressor" to the developing superego system (p. 109).

17. In this section, the word "child" refers to both genders. Sex differences in development are considered in the next section.

18. According to many analysts, the negotiation of the Oedipus complex is considered to be crucial to personality development and to "the orientation of human desire" (Laplanche & Pontalis, p. 283).

19. See Tyson and Tyson, 1990, pp. 207–248, for a comprehensive account of the Oedipus complex and the formation of the superego system.

20. Michael Balint has described female patients who displace ambivalent feelings towards the mother onto other women, and who remain preoccupied with these women.

21. Eliot announces this theme in general terms of the battle between impulse and conscience in the epigraph which introduces the novel:

> "Let thy chief terror be of thine own soul;
> There, 'mid the throng of hurrying desires
> That trample on the dead to seize their spoil,
> Lurks vengeance, footless, irresistible
> As exhalations laden with slow death,
> And o'er the fairest troop of captured joys
> Breathes pallid pestilence".

The thematic content of this verse is repeated late in the novel with a more direct metaphorical reference to Gwendolen's internal world, and this can be related to the dynamics of id, ego and superego:

> ... so it was in Gwendolen's consciousness temptation and dread met and stared like two pale phantoms each seeing itself in the other—each obstructed by its own image; and all the while her fuller self beheld the apparitions and sobbed for deliverance from them. [Eliot, 1876, p. 745]

22. "... Motherly tenderness clung chiefly to her eldest girl, who had been born in her happier time but ... Mrs Davilow was like a frightened child under her daughter's face and voice" (*ibid.*, p. 23).

23. Introduction by Graham Handley, 1984, *Daniel Deronda*, The World's Classics (paperback) edition, Oxford University Press.

24. In her letter to Gwendolen, Lydia Glasher writes like an accusatory and punitive conscience: "You have chosen to injure me and my children . . . you will have your punishment. I desire it with all my Lydia soul . . . The willing wrong you have done me will be your curse". The visual imagery of an accusing apparition and of snakes are associated by Eliot with conscience and its projection. For example, Lydia Glasher makes ". . . a Medusa-apparition before Gwendolen, vindictiveness and jealousy finding relief in an outlet of venom . . . the words had nestled their venomous life within her (pp. 468, 670).

25. Eliot writes,

> The embitterment of hatred . . . [is not necessarily related] to outward causes. Passion is the nature of seed . . . the intensest form of hatred is rooted in fear, which compels to silence and drives vehemence into a constructive vindictiveness, an imaginary annihilation of the detested object, something like . . . hidden rights of vengeance. These intrusive thoughts did not soothe Gwendolen, but add cumulatively to her terror . . . the dread of her husband [is added] to self dread, which urged her to flee from the pursuing images wrought by her pent-up impulse. [pp. 743–744]

26. The degree of suffering that tortures Gwendolen is possible because she "was not a narrow-brained woman who thought selfishness hers by right . . . she had a *root of conscience* in her and the process of purgatory had began for her on . . . earth, she knew she had been wrong" (p. 739).

27. Eliot writes, "He was unique to her among men, because he had impressed her as being not her admirer but her superior: in some mysterious way *he was becoming part of her conscience*" (p. 457).

28. In fact, Gwendolen perceives Deronda as a fearsome conscience / super-ego, expressed by Eliot in vivid metaphorical language as a "*terrible browed angel* from whom she could not think of concealing any deed". She experienced the relationship with him as one in which he demanded truth. His power over her lay in "the raising of self-discontent which could be satisfied only by genuine change" (p. 744).

29. Daniel's actual words are experienced by Gwendolen in a benign, even therapeutic way, in ironic contrast to the bitingly malign power of those of Mrs Glasher quoted earlier. He tells her: "Turn your fear into a safeguard. Keep your dread fixed on the idea of increasing your

remorse. Take your fears as a safeguard. It is like quickness of hearing. It may make consequences passionately present to you" (p. 745).

30.   "I saw him sink . . . I think I did not move . . ." . . . 'the rope!', he called. . . . My heart said 'Die!' and he sank; and I felt 'It is done—I am wicked, I am lost' and I had a rope in my hand. I don't know what I thought—I was leaping away from myself—I would have saved him then. I was leaping away from my crime, and there it was close to me as I fell—there was the dead face—dead, dead. It can never be altered. That was what happened. That was what I did. You know it all. It can never be altered. [pp. 770–771]

In response to this outburst, Daniel observes that Gwendolen's "conscience made her dwell on the determining power of evil thoughts" (p. 771).

31. At this point, Daniel reinforces the demands that Gwendolen's conscience makes on her in that *he demands* that she look at her life as a debt to be paid. He advises that she should "act with that penitential loving purpose you have in your mind", and he assures her, "You will find your life growing like a plant" (p. 851).

32. Again with the use of powerful imagery, Eliot comments on the struggle between impulse and conscience: "poor Gwendolen's memory had been stunned, and all outside the lava lit track of her troubled conscience, and her efforts to get deliverance from it, lay for her in dim forgetfulness" (p. 855). Later in the novel, this statement is expanded:

Gwendolen felt [the habitual feeling of rescue] . . . as she lived through and through again, the terrible history of her temptations, from their first form of illusory self-pleasing when she struggled away from *the hold of conscience,* to their latest form of an urgent hatred dragging her towards its satisfaction, while *she prayed and cried for the help of conscience,* which she had once forsaken. [pp. 881–882]

33. Eliot writes that, when Daniel tells Gwendolen that he is going to marry Mirah, she "began to tremble, her eyes dilated and she cried out 'I said I should be forsaken. I have been a cruel woman. And I am forsaken'". This passage continues that, although "his presence and touch seemed to dispel a horrible vision", she nevertheless began to sob violently. Yet, in spite of her extreme shock and "withered look of grief", she makes some recovery: "I said . . . I said . . . it should be better . . . better with me . . . for having known you" (p. 893).

34. In a final note, Daniel, on the day of his marriage, receives a confirmation of Gwendolen's psychic growth in the form of a letter, which speaks of her determination to make a "new beginning". What is implied, in this passage, by Eliot is how Deronda has contributed towards Gwendolen's development from an earlier egotism towards a greater empathy and a stride towards maturity:

> Do not think of me sorrowfully on your wedding day . . . I have remembered your words—that I may live to be one of the best of women, who make others glad they were born. I do not yet see how that can be, but you know better than I. If it ever becomes true, it will be because you helped me. I only thought of myself, and I made you grieve. It hurts me to think of your grief. You must not grieve any more for me. *It is better—it shall be better with me because I have known you.* [p. 898, my italics]

35. See Kohlberg (1969), who describes the continuous growth of conscience in the school-aged child and beyond.

36. Eliot comments on Sir Hugh Mallinger's attitude to this rumour: ". . . he was pleased with that suspicion; and his imagination had never once been troubled with the way in which the boy himself might be affected, either then or in the future, by the enigmatic aspect of his circumstance" (p. 167).

37. The nature of Daniel's experience is that of an "early rooted feeling that his birth had been attended with injury for which his father was to blame" (p. 304).

38. Eliot writes that he yearned for an "influence that would justify partiality . . . [release him from] roaming like a disembodied spirit, stirred with a vague social passion, but without fixed local habitation to render fellowship real" She describes this state of mind as a "meditative numbness", and she continues, "He found some of the fault in his birth and the way he had been brought up, which had lain no special demands on him and given him no fixed relationship except one of a doubtful kind" (p. 401).

39. The choice of the family name, Dedalus is heavy with metaphorical significance in that the character, Daedalus, in Greek mythology made a labyrinth (i.e., a maze, a complicated structure with many passages and hard to find a way through without guidance), in which he finds himself imprisoned. He then invents a pair of wings that enable him to escape the labyrinth.

40. Parnell (1846–1891) was the great advocate of parliamentary home rule for Ireland, and of land reform. Dante's bad opinion of him arose from

his adultery, which caused the Catholic clergy to turn against him and others to experience conflicting loyalties. Her final remark anticipates and associates to Joyce's later account of the Catholic "Hell", in which the devil and devilish "fiends" are prominent. Joyce writes, "Hell is a straight and dark and foul smelling prison, an abode of demons and lost souls" (1992, p. 128).

41. In this respect, it is interesting to compare Freud's comments on "Jewish guilt", and therefore the "Jewish superego".

> Paul ... [called this sense of guilt] "original sin" ... a crime against God ... [that could] only be atoned for by death ... a sense of guilt rose from hostility [against the father and by implication against God] ... a bad conscience for having sinned against God and not ceasing to sin. [*Moses and Monotheism*, pp. 86–87, 134]

42. The account of "the Catholic superego" ("death, judgement, hell and heaven") through the eye of an obsessional priest, is horrific and terrifying. Its threats cause "spiritless despair" and trembling in Stephen: "the preacher blew death into his soul".

43. Joyce's account of this episode has a significantly ironic and humorous element.

44. The portrayal of Stephen's development is an ironic one with a critical dimension. For example, an aspect of Stephen's growing up is clearly marked by the exaggeration of a person newly converted and by his superior airs. His transformation from the devout Catholic to the artist is idealized, and is a romanticized version of people's ordinary lives in Dublin. Blamires (1984) has noted that Joyce's description of Stephen's exile is suggestive of a *second infancy*.

CHAPTER FOUR

The object and the superego

"True morality begins when the internalised criticism, now embodied in the standard exacted by the superego, coincides with the ego's perception of its own fault"

(Freud, A., 1936)

"Psychology is a study of the relationships of the individual to its objects, whilst . . . psychopathology [is] . . . a study of the relationship of the ego to its internalised objects"

(Fairbairn, 1952)

I t has been observed that Freud's formulation of the superego was "the true beginning of sound object relations theory" and, therefore, the birth of two-person psychology (Coltart, 1992, p. 50). My discussion of object relations is limited in two ways. It focuses on the development of classical ideas by a few influential psychoanalysts working mainly in the UK, and it considers some of their contributions only in so far as they are relevant to classical superego theory.[1]

12 50

1.52

The Contemporary Freudian tradition

However, before considering these particular analysts, and in order to put their work in the general context of superego investigation, I will discuss the important contribution to theory, and research, of analysts associated with the Anna Freud Centre.

Anna Freud, herself, regarded the system superego as crucial in the formation of neurosis, and its analysis, as an essential part of therapeutic work. Following her father's theoretical views, she regarded the superego structure as appearing relatively late in development, between the phallic phase and latency, and as becoming established after the Oedipus complex (i.e., between three and four years). Only when the complex was "overcome" was the superego formed (i.e., between five and six years).

She describes superego anxiety, anxiety of conscience and the sense of guilt as powerful influences in children, and in adults. She considered that the superego works by setting an ideal standard that restricts the expression of sexuality and aggression. However, when the ego responds by obeying the superego's orders, and acts defensively, it could become "incapable of enjoyment".

> The superego [is] a redoubtable force . . . the mischief maker . . . it sets up an ideal standard, according to which sexuality is prohibited and aggression pronounced to be antisocial . . . [this] impels us to pay special attention to . . . the analysis of the superego. [Freud, A., 1936, p. 55]

An analytic task, therefore, was to relieve the ego by controlling the superego's demands; i.e., by seeking "a diminution in its power, a modification of its severity . . .". Given this stress on the significance of the superego, it followed that she used the concept widely in her work, and this is evident in many of her case descriptions (*ibid.*, pp. 116–118, 125–128).

She also applied her well-established theory of "identification with the aggressor" to the ongoing development of the superego system, and related it to the process of "introject formation" at the toddler stage (see Chapter Three). For example, she describes how the toddler identifies with the mother saying "No!" and how this stimulates a development in which the toddler says "No! No!" to him-/herself.

In her many comments on the superego, Anna Freud consistently draws attention to its immaturity in much of childhood, in the sense that it does not function as an independent psychic structure and it lacks "autonomy" (Holder, 2005).[2]

In the epigraph to this chapter, Anna Freud indicates how the latency child is only gradually able to achieve a less parent-influenced and more autonomous superego. For her, therefore, the child's early superego becomes substantially altered in the course of later development.

In her comments on adolescence, she notes that when the young person in his/her thoughts and actions is able to move beyond the internalized, parental representations, there may result a very distressed state of mind, and she refers to this as "inner object loss". She further suggests that sometimes the way these painful feelings are managed is by displacement of the emotional ties and superego functions onto a "strong, idealised group leader".[3]

In relation to therapeutic work, Anna Freud particularly stressed the effect of the child's dependency on the parents as present and real "objects" in his/her life. This social situation was, therefore, a limiting factor in the analytic work with the child, and required special consideration. For her, the analyst became a "new love object", who temporarily offered a "new ego ideal" to the child, thus displacing the parental ideal. It followed that, in Anna Freud's view, the analytic enterprise, in addition to work with the child, required parental casework that aimed at modification of the parents' attitudes to the child (Holder, 2005, p. 82).[4]

I turn now to the contribution of those analysts who worked in close association with Anna Freud, and were inspired and trained by her. Joseph and Anne-Marie Sandler were particularly prominent members of this group, which, beginning in the 1950s, carried out extensive research with children, including into the system superego (see Sandler & Sandler, 1998). In their discussions of this work, they drew attention, for example, to the child's "feeling of being loved" when the ego and superego were in harmony, and thus to the positive effects of the approval function of the superego. They also described the child's constant need for "affirmation", "nourishment", and "reassurance", from the object, which they considered were important contributors to "the background of safety". Such feelings were thought to be at the root of the subject's attachment to the superego introject. In this connection, they also point out how some analysts may use interpretations that unintentionally reinforce negative aspects of the patient's superego, for example, its intolerance.

In an attempt to integrate the idea of internal object relations into what they refer to as "acceptable psychoanalytic theory", the Sandlers defined a structure as: "an enduring organization which may or may not be involved in current mental processes to a significant extent, but nevertheless persists and can be brought into use when appropriate" (ibid., p. 124).

With this in mind, the superego (along with the id and the ego) is described as a "macrostructure" that requires careful theoretical clarification (ibid., p. 124, where the Sandlers describe the background of this research).

The Sandlers describe the nature ("the fabric") of the child's superego system as partly composed of imperatives (the "Do's and Don'ts", the "Shoulds and Should nots"). Such commands, together with the moral standards, ideals, and wished for goals, that have been handed down by the parents, and other significant figures in the child's life, come to form the superego system. They point out that, since these constituents come from diverse sources, they do not necessarily form a consistent set of values, but are rather "a full and harmonized organisation of divergent trends" (Tyson & Tyson, 1990, p. 201).

As a step towards unravelling, and clarifying, the conceptual complexity that this formulation clearly implies, they proposed that a distinction be drawn between an introject and an ideal. In their view, the term "introject" should be limited to "directives, admonitions or prohibitions" that have been internalized, and the ideal should be limited to the individual's "wished for standards". However, they also make the assumption that, "in reality", these rules and wishes function together.

As a result of a further investigation of "the ego ideal", they suggest that, in the light of its complexity, the concept should be subdivided into *ideal object representations, ideal child representations* and *ideal self representations*. They describe the "ideal object representations" as early formations in which the parents are perceived as perfect and omnipotent. These early impressions are noted as having remarkably persistent standards against which later perceptions are measured. The "ideal child representations" are composed of actual parental standards, morals, goals, and ideals, that become mixed up with parental fantasies and wishes for the child (e.g., "the child my father wishes me to be"). They found that, since these representations were mainly derived from the parental superegos, it followed that, if the parents showed inconsistency, the child was likely to internalize the faulty superego problem.

Sandler and Sandler describe the "ideal self representation" (itself a complex conscious and unconscious structure with several sources) as "the self I would like to be", and they understood this construction to be more sophisticated than that of the introjects of early infancy (Sandler & Sandler, 1998, p. 12).

Lastly in this section, I turn to certain analysts, and child and adolescent therapists, who were initially trained in the Contemporary Freudian tradition and became particularly interested in the developmental problems of children, and in the role of the analyst as a "developmental object". Ann Hurry (1998) writes:

> I found myself acting as a developmental object, contradicting his view of me and enabling him to feel safe enough to use interpretation . . . when Tom was ready to catch up on the lacunae in development . . . I interacted with him in the way that I felt he needed. [p. 78]

Hurry has provided an example of the work of this kind that is directly relevant to superego theory. She describes the case of a ten-year-old patient, "Tom", in which the work was aimed at mitigating the severity of the superego attacks on the self. She saw the therapeutic aim as one of undoing a "developmental hitch". In a clinical description, she refers to a game, called "Heaven's Gate", in which the young patient was able to examine, and work through, the sources of his guilt feelings. In the course of the treatment, Tom had given himself the role of "the gate keeper" to "Heaven". In his play, he made the analyst into "a very bad person" who was punished by being sent to "Hell". Hurry describes how Tom, by a process of externalization and identification with the cruel superego, had attempted to avoid its condemnation.

As the analysis progressed, she describes how the patient's capacity to "play" improved and he became able to allow others into "Heaven's gate". This was a development in the treatment that, she notes, seemed to indicate the establishment of a *more benign superego,* which, she says, implied a growing confidence that Tom felt himself to be more acceptable to the analyst. She points to evidence that this gradual process of modifying the severe super-ego (indicated by signs of improvement, e.g., the setting-up of a half-way house to which the analyst was sent for a trial and judge-ment, rather than being sent straight to Hell) was a significant feature of the analysis. This growth in Tom of a capacity for discrim-ination also reflected the beginning of a greater kindliness of the superego towards the self.

In her concluding section, Hurry comments that, by the time Tom had left his junior school, he was more in touch with his affects. This suggested that his previous pattern of automatic "superego condemnation" had given place to a more benign, philo-sophical and questioning attitude (*ibid.,* p. 98). This change clearly indicates a significant growth in superego development in adoles-cence towards greater maturity, in the sense that the more primtive, condemning superego had given way to a more age-appropriate, and benign, rational examination of morality and "the rights and wrongs of life".

Rose Edgcumbe has written at length about the use of "the diag-nostic profile" in the gathering of an important body of research, by workers from the Anna Freud Centre, on ego and superego devel-opment in children (Edgcumbe, 2000, pp. 83–101; 102–105).

She summarizes the use of the profile in establishing whether the nature of the superego is age-adequate in so far as the child is, or is not, dependent on external sources, and to what degree "inde-pendence" has been achieved. The profile also assesses various qualities of the superego, e.g., its harshness, severity, benignity, punitiveness, etc.

Edgcumbe discusses the Sandlers' attempt to distinguish the ego and the self and provides interesting case material as illustration (*ibid.,* p. 103). She describes the case of "George", in which a regres-sion of "drives, ego and superego" had remained in the analysis as a long and intractable defence. In this example, Edgcumbe notes that analytic work on conflicts, and the patient's identification with more benign internal objects, had resulted in a "more balanced superego including some benign rewarding and aim-giving aspects" (see also Freeman (1998), Ekins and Freeman (1994), and Holder (2005), for further discussion and case illustrations).

The object-relations theorists

The object-relations analysts had certain theoretical views in common, but they nevertheless held radically different ideas from one another, so that no unified theory was ever to emerge. What they held in common was the significance to be given to the idea of "human relationship", the psychological importance of the "self", and the quest for the "self" to make contact with the "other". The latter was considered to be the basic developmental task of becoming a human being.

In order to construct a self, the individual needed to interact with, and gain experience of, another self. However, at the earliest developmental stage, this interaction would be with a part of another self (i.e., a "part object"). This approach to human development was, therefore, in contrast to classical theory, which defined the object (i.e., its mental representation) as that towards which the biological drive aimed. Nevertheless, pointers to this new direction can be found in Freud's work and that of other classical analysts. For example, the notion of the superego as having been formed by the internalization of parental attitudes, and values, was clearly a forerunner of the concept of the internal object.

These object-relations theorists posited the existence of an inner world that consists of a complex system of internal relationships. This conception implied that mental representations of the self were in dynamic interaction with one another, at different conscious and unconscious levels. In this theoretical scheme, the "person" is conceptualized as living a twofold existence between an internal and external world, which are in constant interaction with, and influenced by, each other. This new emphasis was to give psychoanalytic research a fresh focus and direction, which centred on the relationship between the ego and its internalized object.

However, as has been mentioned above, there were certain significant disagreements among these analysts, which are now discussed. These differences centred especially on the meaning and function of "objects", the nature of the internal world, and the relationship between the "internal" and the "external". It should be emphasized, however, that, in this new direction of research, certain fundamental classical concepts, such as conflict and anxiety, were retained, and that these remained central to psychoanalytic exploration, although other concepts were questioned, modified, or disregarded (Buckley, 1986).

The Kleinian tradition

It was Melanie Klein who, as a result of her pioneering analytic work with very young children, described in great detail an inner world of objects and unconscious phantasy. (For discussions on the meaning of "phantasy", see Bott-Spillius, 1988; Hinshelwood, 1989; Hayman, 1989; Isaacs, 1948; Segal, 1978.)

Klein's research sought to demonstrate that the baby, in earliest infancy, was object-related (i.e., the baby was, from the beginning, related to a representation of the breast as a part-object). In her view, this rich world of phantasy interacted with, and dominated, the infant's perception of the outer world.

In the light of this research, Klein proposed substantial revisions to the classical theory of the superego. She observed, and reported on, pre-oedipal phantasies, and anxieties, in children under the age of two, and concluded that a primitive form of the superego was in evidence in the first year of life and, therefore, much earlier than had been assumed previously. She described the infant as having internalized a very *primitive, infantile superego* consisting of "part-objects", which holds sway over and greatly influences the *primitive, infantile ego*.

She also suggested that the Oedipus complex had early roots, and this theorizing led, in turn, to the new formulations of the paranoid–schizoid and depressive "positions". The Kleinian infant initially experienced "persecutory anxiety" (i.e., the fear of being attacked by projected "bad" part-objects) and was later subject to "depressive anxiety" (i.e., the fear of what the infant fantasizes his "badness" could do to "whole" objects; see Chapter Three).

It was the concept of a "position" and Klein's revision of Freud's theory of anxiety that helped her to define, and clarify, the nature of the structure of the ego and, in turn, the superego (Klein, 1934; Segal, 1978).

As her work progressed, it also became clear that the early primitive superego, conceptualized as an "internal phantasy object", had severe and powerful destructive qualities, which acted unconsciously to punish the child/adult in savage ways. In her view, Freud's formulation of a superego that originated with the resolution of the Oedipal complex was the last stage of a more complex development, and one which was associated with part, as well as whole, object relationships.

Segal writes, "In the oral sadistic phase, the child attacks his mother's breast and incorporates it as both destroyed and destructive—'a bad persecuting internal breast'. This is the *earliest root of the persecuting and sadistic aspects of the superego*" (1978, p. 4, my italics).

Klein's research into infantile conflict, anxiety, and defence, also led to a re-evaluation of the role of aggression in the formation of the inner structures of the ego and the superego. According to her, the phantasy life of the infant was due, partly to the introjection of a parental figure, and partly to a distortion arising from the infant's own projections. In illustration of this view, Segal has provided an example of a patient whose aggression was projected into the father, and she shows how the introjection of a representation of the father then formed the superego.

Segal illustrates this projection of the subject in a dream from a patient who was a naval officer. The dream contained an admiral/father/superego, who was strong and frightening. However, the severity of the superego was due to the patient's projection of hostility into the father, and the reintrojection of the father formed his superego.

Another of Klein's observations concerned the significant role of envy in human development, and how this had implications for superego formation. In an illustration of this idea, Segal provides an example in which her male patient's superego was experienced as envious and spoiling, and this led to attacks on the self and its achievements (see also case illustration in Chapter One). Segal describes a patient's dream in which he is walking together with, and feeding, a "dinosaurus" who has also eaten everybody else up. The patient is frightened that he too will be eaten, when he runs out of food for the dinosaurus. Segal writes that further analysis revealed the analyst as the internalized father, and pointed to the significance of the patient's unconscious envy.

In the description of her work, Klein uses the term *infantile superego*, which she describes as having powerful effects on the weaker, more vulnerable *infantile ego*. In her commentary, Segal suggests how, in favourable circumstances, the analytic process may act to curb these excessive demands.

In my own work, I have used the case material of Mrs Blue to emphasize powerful unconscious guilt, and how this led to the severe punishment of her own body (see Chapter Two).

Before leaving this very schematic and brief summary of Melanie Klein's views on the significance of internal objects, and of the system superego, it is helpful to summarize some of her differences with classical theory and, in particular, with Anna Freud's position discussed earlier. The views of the two pioneers on the timing, formation, and structure, of the system superego were fundamentally different.[5]

Klein's emphasis was on the great strength, power, severity, and cruelty of the *early, primitive superego,* and on how this was the basis of child psychopathology. It follows that the control of this very early formation, and the undoing of its power over the child's mental life was a primary aim of child analysis. According to Klein, both the Oedipus complex and the early formation of the superego system begin with the weaning process. Another crucial difference from the clasical view was that the formation of the superego *preceded* the Oedipus complex rather than *overcame* it, and this change in sequence had important consequences. For example, when the one-year-old suffers oral (and anal) frustration, the superego could be conceptualized in phantasy as something that "bites, devours, and cuts" the maternal object.

In her early papers, Klein expressed the view that "There is only one superego which is firmly rooted in the child and whose nature is immutable". This notion, then, was that of a basic core structure, originating in primitive projections and identifications, and relatively immovable. In contrast to Anna Freud, this view was suggestive of an autonomous structure that was formed at an early stage of childhood, and that was not essentially different to the superego of adulthood (Holder, 2005, p. 87).[6]

Post-Kleinian developments

I wish now to consider some examples of post-Kleinian developments that, considered together, form a considerable body of research into the superego. In a comment on the pioneer analytic research with schizophrenics in the 1950s, Bott-Spillius (1988) has drawn attention to the work of those analysts who found much confirmation of Klein's views of an early and persecuting superego.

In this section, I begin with Wilfred Bion, although, strictly speaking, he always disclaimed that he belonged to any "Group". However, it is convenient to consider his important contribution here since he was much influenced by, and made exceptional use of, Kleinian theory. For example, his observations on the psychotic mind drew upon Klein's theory of a primitive superego. He also applied several of her concepts to an understanding of his own analytic findings (e.g., part-object relations, the paranoid–schizoid and depressive positions, and the concepts of envy, splitting, and projective identification). He further developed these ideas, in the light of his work with borderline and psychotic patients, and applied them to his theory of thinking (O'Shaughnessy, 2005).

What particularly interested Bion was what he termed *the moral impulse*, and what he sought to demonstrate was how, at a primitive level, this *basic morality* could become corrupted, perverted, and employed against the self. He also described the extremely primitive nature of the early superego, which he found was linked with severe pathology. He considered it important to differentiate this primitive superego from more developed, sophisticated, and rational *systems of morality*. He writes as follows:

> The moral impulse is extremely primitive—the moral system, the conscience, cannot be appreciated unless its primitive nature is recognised . . . terms such as "*superego*" suggest something above everything else. It is more likely [to be something] . . . "*underneath, basic, fundamental*". [2000, p. 24]

He continues by suggesting that it is easy to rationalize, and therefore under-emphasize, this primitive source, if engaged in constructing rational, sophisticated, moral systems.

Bion describes the features of the psychotic personality, which he understood to always co-exist with the non-psychotic parts. In comparing the two, he linked psychotic functioning with the infant's situation in the paranoid–schizoid position, in which the tendency was to substitute destructive attacks on the ego for the capacity to repress.[7]

He further describes psychotic functioning as formed via a process of pathological projective identification, and he relates this to a container–contained model. The normal projective process has become pathological in the sense that there occurs a violent fragmentation and evacuation of the mental apparatus into multiple fragments (i.e., splitting). In psychosis, this pathological process is accompanied by the infusion of fragments into objects in the external world, forming *bizarre objects*. These may be a "hotch-potch" of fragments made up from split-off parts of the self (ego, superego) and aspects of "real" objects. Bion refers to these as *beta elements*. In this way, the particles of personality are transformed into "things".

In normal development, the infant projects his "uncontrollable emotions" ("the contained") into the "good breast" ("the container") and receives them back from the object in a form that can be coped with, taken in, and digested. "The infant projects a part of his psyche, especially his uncontrolled emotions ('the contained') only to receive them back 'detoxified' and in a more tolerable form" (Bion, 2000, p. 28).

Bion shows how, when this relationship is suffused with envy, the "elements" of the relationship become emptied of meaning and vitality, and the normal growth process is inhibited or destroyed. When this pathological situation occurs, the psychotic part of the personality becomes dominant. In his account, he describes how this process leads to the formation of a powerful, and highly destructive, *Super* ego in the mind.

According to Bion, in psychotic functioning, the normally developing superego has become corrupted and acts in a perverse sense, in that it omnipotently opposes "learning from experience". This *Super* ego (also aptly referred to, by Horatio Etchegoyen, as a *super-super ego*) acts in opposition to scientific thinking and development, "external and psychic reality", and "normal" ideas of right and wrong. In other words, it has become a perverse superego guiding, and guided by, a corrupt morality. Bion writes:

> It emerges from the confusing consequences of excessive pathological projective identification, and its "moral" criteria could be defined as an affirmation of destructive superiority, a determination to possess in order to stop what is possessed from having an existence of its own. [2000, p. 29]

Although the normal superego and the *Super* ego both initiate feelings of guilt, the latter is responsible for a much greater degree of persecution. It is this power that is put to use by the psychotic part of the personality. Bion gives illuminating illustrations of this persecutory process in his case material, for example, in *Second Thoughts* (1967).

According to Bion, especially characteristic of psychotic functioning is the "attack on linking". This includes the links with the analyst and the analytic process, and all the linking relationships of normal, healthy growth and development. Those residual links that may survive this destructive process, tend to be of a perverse, cruel, sterile nature. He associates these with "arrogance" (an especially significant concept for Bion), "stupidity", and what he calls "obstinate curiosity", and he refers these traits to the influence of an internal object (i.e., the highly pathological *Super* ego).

The source of the psychotic personality lies, at least in part, in the deficiencies of the container. In whole-object terms, what the infant has encountered is "a mother who was unable to perform her function of receiving, containing, and modifying, the violent emotions projected by the child" (Grinberg, Sor, & Tabak de Bianchedi, 1993, p. 30).

In other words, a *Super* ego of this kind may become established when something goes very badly wrong between mother and infant, and this results in a part of the self acting in opposition to, and severely damaging, the rest of the self. Bion (1959) writes, "the early development of the superego is affected by this kind of mental functioning i.e. an attack on the link between the infant and the breast . . . [an incapacity] to introject projective identifications" (p. 107). This failure results in "an object which, when installed in the patient, exercises the function of a severe and ego destructive superego".

I turn next to the pioneering research of Herbert Rosenfeld (1952), who, in introducing his work with schizophrenic patients, discusses Klein's account of how the infant projects libidinal and aggressive impulses on to external objects, which, at first, are his mother's breasts. In Rosenfeld's view, the infant creates, in phantasy, images of a "good" and "bad" breast, which are then introjected, and this process contributes to the growth of the ego and superego. If, in the first few months of the infant's life, persecutory phantasies predominate over "good" object representations, the core of the primitive superego will develop a persecutory character.

A second feature that may contribute to the persecutory super-ego is the development of *idealized "good" objects*. The infant's developmental move to the depressive position is accompanied by the fear that the good object will be destroyed, together with a wish to preserve it inside. A fear that this will not be achieved marks the superego conflict of the depressive position. It is when this situation cannot be worked through, Rosenfeld suggests, that regression to the paranoid–schizoid position will take place.

Rosenfeld gives an interesting account of a patient who, all his life, had avoided the experience of guilt and anxiety, so that "he couldn't feel fear". The patient's superego had attacked his ego, via powerful evacuative projective identification, and Rosenfeld shows how this had led to the ego's disintegration. He reports that this patient "felt quite worn out" by the enormous demands of his conscience. In his description of the analytic process, Rosenfeld shows how the patient was able to get in touch with a "helpful" superego part of himself, and how this gradually enabled him to take some control over "the self". The patient also became more willing "to accept and face" his superego (i.e., "to look at his inner object").

From the theoretical viewpoint, Rosenfeld was able to make a comparison between the superego of Klein's paranoid–schizoid position and that of the depressive position. The former is variously described as cruel, sadistic, unrelenting, murderous, etc., whereas the latter, although accusatory and critical, is less severe and savage (i.e., it merely "accuses, complains, suffers, and makes demands for reparation").[8]

More recent post-Kleinian contributions

Edna O'Shaughnessy (1999) has provided a more recent account of normal and abnormal forms of the superego. Following Klein, Bion, and Rosenfeld, she illustrates the savage nature of a very early, primitive introject that is "deeply split off" and engaged in attacks on the ego–self and its objects. This is described as a superego which "stood apart . . . unmodified by the normal processes of

growth". In a paper noteworthy for the clarity of the clinical interaction, she discusses the implications for the analysis of a transference in which *abnormal relating occurs* "superego to . . . superego",
and how this situation can lead to an impasse in the analytic
process (*ibid,.* p. 863).

She describes a patient, Mrs A, who criticized, hated, condemned,
and rejected, the analyst and the "set-up", and who could not gain
any recognition, or insight, into her projections or severe difficulties.
The patient projected this critique and then experienced the analyst
as severely critical of, and hostile towards, her. O'Shaughnessy
understood the clinical material as an example of the functioning of
Bion's *Super* ego (which acts as an "envious assertion of moral supe-
riority without any morals"). In this case study, the *Super* ego was
engaged in attacks on healthy linking with the object and the ego,
and on normal superego development.

O'Shaughnessy infers, from the evidence of the transference and
countertransference, the presence in the patient of an early maternal internal object that "condemns the patient for not matching her
anticipated ideal". In the transference, the patient experienced a
dissatisfaction as coming from the analyst towards her, as a "repetition of her infantile distress".

She comments on the impasse as follows: "Mrs A is by turns
terrified by and identified with an abnormal superego . . . [a stuck
situation in which] no psychic work can take place" (p. 863).

After a further detailed description of her work with a second
patient, a "Mr B",[9] she arrives at the following conclusion:

> In my view, because of the antagonism between the pathological
> superego and the operation of normal ethics, escaping its clutches
> and regaining contact with an object with normal superego aspects
> are among the more significant analytic events in clinical work with
> patients like Mrs A and Mr B. [O'Shaughnessy, 1999, p. 869]

An extensive and interesting exploration of the system superego
has been contributed by Ronald Britton (2003) in which the author
examines the relationship between the ego and the superego
systems. Starting from the pioneering theoretical work of Klein and
Bion, he compares the two systems and their interaction.

In his examination, he contrasts two kinds of "authority". The
first he describes as arising from "judgement based on experience",

and on the individual's "reality testing", and these functions he allocates to the ego. He then contrasts this with "moral" authority, which is based on parental and ancestral (especially cultural and religious) values, and it is this that he links to the domain of the superego.

In a re-evaluation of the ego–superego systems, Britton allocates greater theoretical significance to the ego, and seems to go beyond Freud and connects with Fairbairn's theories (see below). He concludes that "self-observation" and "self-judgement" are ego functions (i.e., he makes a distinction between *realistic* observation and judgement and *moral* observation and judgement). In health, he suggests that the "emancipated" ego of the mature adult will be able to judge the superego (i.e., an individual can judge his own conscience). According to Britton, in the growth process, a person who has successfully negotiated the depressive position has changed the nature of his guilt feelings from superego punishment to remorse, which Britton defines as "an affect of the ego accompanied by a wish to make reparation" (*ibid.*, p. 72). However, in illness (e.g., in obsessional neurosis), the developmental process has been reversed, in that the ego has become the slave of the superego.

He also discusses the important theoretical issue as to whether ". . . an internal object [is] necessarily part of the superego"[10]. He comments that "all internal objects *might* operate as the superego and that there is a great deal of difference when they do if they are hostile or tyrannical . . . I see the position of superego as a place in the psyche to be occupied . . . [rather than] as an inherent structure" (*ibid.*, p.74, see also Hinshelwood, 1989, pp. 94–111).

Britton concludes that: "*the third position of triangular space—that of self observation—is within the ego*" (original italics). It is, however, vulnerable to invasion by the superego, which substitutes its own language of self-reproach, self-deprecation, and self-admonition, for self appraisal. (For a more comprehensive discussion, see Britton, 2003.)

When the ego is thus invaded, a new language of morality has been put in place.

Finally, before concluding this section, I wish to mention the short introduction to the superego concept entitled *The Superego*, by Priscilla Roth, published in 2001. This work provides a useful summary of some of the basic issues involved, and is written with the lay reader in mind. It offers a brief, but pithy, introduction to the place of the concept in psychoanalytic theory, and it poses and responds to some interesting and relevant questions, such as "What good is a superego if it only makes you feel bad?". The illustrations from literature, and other sources, are particularly vivid and enlightening.

The Independent tradition

I begin with a summary of the very original work of Ronald Fairbairn, who attempted to set out a comprehensive theory of object-relations that was independent of classical drive theory. With regard to the superego and the Oedipus complex, it should be noted that Fairbairn was critical of classical theory. However, he allocated certain superego functions, initially, to what he termed the *internal saboteur* and, later, to the *moral defence* (Fairbairn, 1952, 1958, 1963).[11] This will be briefly considered below in so far as it is relevant to my own exploration of the superego.

Of all object relation theories, his was perhaps the most revolutionary. His work on schizoid mental states led him to reject Freud's instinct theory and the concept of the id, and to question the pleasure principle and the hedonistic theory of motivation. He concluded that "the object and not gratification is the ultimate aim of libidinal striving".

His revision of classical theory gave a central position to the ego ("the pristine personality of the child consists of a unitary dynamic ego"). According to Fairbairn, the infant has an ego at birth, whole and undivided, and was therefore innately equipped with a built-in system of internal defences which were linked up with the object. The infant, "a libidinal 'I'", was, therefore, pre-programmed to relate to "the other", i.e., another libidinal "I", and was primarily "object-seeking" rather than "pleasure-seeking".

It followed, for Fairbairn, that, at the deepest motivational level, the infant strove to make contact with "the other", and that the most powerful human anxiety was associated with separation from, and loss of love of, "the other".[12]

Unlike Freud and Klein (but in line with the views of Winnicott and Balint), Fairbairn regarded aggression as a secondary phenomenon, which only occurred when the striving for libidinal contact was thwarted. He thus rejected the idea of a death instinct, or of a primary destructive drive.

In his view, it was only after birth, and as a result of the normal stresses and frustrations of ordinary life, that there occurred a division of the ego–self. The splits that occurred within the self also set parts of the self against each other. For Fairbairn, a fundamental primary division occurred in all human development, which he termed "the schizoid position". He considered that every individual person was faced with the task of negotiating this position, and it was how this situation came to be resolved that structured the ego–self (Fairbairn, 1944, p. 90).

Fairbairn's developmental theory consists of three parts, and each of these relates to degrees of separation between self and other. At the earliest stage, called "infantile dependence", when the dependence is total, the carer is bound to fail, and this failure results in the splitting of the ego and the creation of the "schizoid position". For Fairbairn, this developmental challenge was a norm of all human development. The pathological conditions of schizophrenia and depression were disturbances that demonstrated the individual's failure to resolve the schizoid position (Fairbairn, 1946).[13]

The following developmental stage is described as one of "transitional dependence". This is one in which the infant adopts one or other "technique" (the phobic, obsessional, hysterical, or paranoid) as a way of managing the psychic situation (*ibid.*, pp.145–146).[14]

The psychopathology of this transitional stage centres on obsessional neurosis, paranoid states, hysterical phenomena and phobic symptoms (see Fairbairn, 1944, 1946, 1952).

The third stage, he called one of "mature dependence", and this involves the achievement of a successful separation in the sense that the other's separateness is now firmly recognized by the self (*ibid.*, p. 145).[15]

Fairbairn (1952) discusses in detail the nature of the infant's psychic withdrawal from its "object", i.e., carer. This involves a basic conflict between the fundamental urge to relate and certain "primary trauma" which relate to the absence of, or loss of, love (see Gomez, 1997; Guntrip, 1961).

In contrast to Freud, Fairbairn's account of the Oedipal complex focuses on emotional contact rather than instinctual gratification, and he regarded the complex as a cultural phenomenon and a product of the infant's process of "relating" at the transitional stage. He describes the child's dynamics of relating to its parents in terms of exciting and rejecting objects, and understands the intensity (and psychopathology when it occurs) of the Oedipal situation, as associated with earlier stages of deprivation, inner splitting, and parental failure of emotional contact, on the one hand, or of seductiveness, on the other. For him, it is environmental factors that interact with the child's defences and his/her use of physical excitement (Fairbairn, 1944, pp. 119–125).

Fairbairn was also critical of Freud's use of the concept of the superego, and of classical "phase theory", pointing out certain inconsistencies from a developmental point of view. From 1943 onwards, he regarded the superego as an agent of what he referred to as "the moral defence" (i.e., a complex of internal structures that originated in the splitting of the self at the earliest developmental phase).

According to Fairbairn, the normal infant has to adapt to frustrations caused by unmet needs. To do this, he separates off the "bad" experiences, and relocates the "them" inside the self. In this way, an ambivalent relationship is internalized in that an "internal object" is formed with "good" and "bad" parts. The good part remains connected to *the central ego*, but the bad part is further subdivided into a *libidinal ego* and an *anti-libidinal ego*. The libidinal ego (a fragment of the original ego that has been disavowed) is attached to an exciting object. The anti-libidinal ego (also a fragment of the original ego) is now bonded to the rejecting object. It is this anti-libidinal ego that, emerging from repression, attacks the self. It is this relocation of "badness" that Fairbairn refers to as "the moral defence". His suggestion is that, when the infant internalizes his "good" objects, they assume a *superego role*. He says that from the infant's standpoint it is as if ". . . it is better to be a sinner in a world ruled by God than to live in a world ruled by the Devil" (Fairbairn, 1943, pp. 66–67).

Because the source of this structure was in early infancy, it could not be associated with the later development of the Freudian Oedipus complex and the classical superego. In Fairbairn's 1952 publication, there are a number of references to the "superego", suggesting a continuous struggle to re-establish the ideas relating to the concept in his own theoretical formulations.

In his 1944 paper on the revision of endo-psychic structure, the superego has given way (though the concept itself is not abandoned) to "the internal saboteur" (Fairbairn, 1944, p. 101). This structure largely corresponds to the superego in function, but it also differs in that it is an ego structure rather than an internal object. It is also more complex than the classical idea, since it is a "compound of the superego and its associated object". An even more crucial difference is that it is "devoid of all moral significance" (*ibid.*, pp. 106–107). The superego concept is nevertheless retained by Fairbairn, because he considered it necessary to account for the sense of guilt. He refers to it as a "naturalized alien, within the realm of the individual mind, an immigrant from outer reality". In substituting the internal saboteur for the superego, Fairbairn differs from the Kleinian description of the primitive superego, since he understands the structure to have originated "at a higher level of mental organisation than that at which the internal saboteur operates" (1944, pp. 107–108).

In his paper, *Object relations and dynamic structure* (1946), Fairbairn arrived at what he called "a new psychology of dynamic structure" in which the "central ego" corresponded to Freud's ego, the "libidinal ego" to the id, and the "internal saboteur" to the superego. These are considered as "dynamic structures" that have originated from the splitting of the single, "unitary dynamic" ego structure that was present at the beginning of life. (In a footnote to his 1949 paper *Steps in the development of an object-relations theory of the personality* (p. 160), Fairbairn incorporates "the ego ideal" as the "basis for the establishment of moral values in the inner world".)

In summary, Fairbairn considers each aspect of Freud's tripartite model as a dynamic structure in its own right. With this in mind, he found that the superego, as described by Freud, was conceptually unbalanced (see Fairbairn-Birtles and Scharf, 1994, p. 137).

It should also be noted that, in his revised model of the mind, a sense of guilt has resolved itself into a defence against relationships with bad objects (1949, p. 156). In a case illustration of unconscious guilt related to oral–sadistic wishes, Fairbairn writes:

> the superego is built up in layers corresponding to stages in oedipal development. It also revealed that the nucleus of the superego is pregenital in origin, belongs to an oral level and must therefore become established during the oral phase. [Fairbairn, 1931, p. 221]

In comparing Klein's (1948) description of a multiplicity of good and bad internal objects with Freud's idea of a single internal object (the superego), Fairbairn says that she demonstrates that, "in health", it is this multiplicity that gives rise to the superego. Building on her idea, he evolves a revised model of the psychic apparatus (an "endopsychic situation") in which each ego structure is assigned an appropriate object, and arrives at three groupings: (1) "a central ego" cathecting "an ideal object"; (2) "a libidinal ego" cathecting "an exciting object"; and (3) "an anti-libidinal ego" cathecting "a rejecting object" (Fairbairn-Birtles & Scharff, 1994, pp. 137–138).

In this revised model, the superego has "largely" been replaced by the anti-libidinal ego, a revision that he considered had certain theoretical advantages over what he considered were the inconsistencies of Freud's superego theory. (See also Guntrip, 1961, 1968, 1971; Kernberg, 1975; Scharff, 1994.)

I turn last in this chapter to discuss, and summarize, Donald Winnicott's contributions to superego theory. Winnicott was well acquainted with Fairbairn's work and was critical of some of his central ideas (e.g., primary identification), which he found contradictory. In his view, at the very earliest, primitive developmental stage, that of primary narcissism, in which there was a merging between the "Me" and "Not Me", there was no differentiation between subject and object. It was, therefore, difficult to conceive of the infant seeking a "relationship" between the two. In Winnicott's view, Freud was correct that what the infant sought was pleasure; that is, that the libido was "pleasure" orientated rather than "object" seeking.

Winnicott's concept of the superego is based on the theoretical views of Freud, Anna Freud, and Melanie Klein, but is also strikingly original. His idea of a "true morality" (see epigraph to Chapter Three, p. 45) is embedded in the earliest mother–infant relationship, the time for him of "primary narcissism", from which the infant, "in health" will later emerge to develop a capacity for a *sense of guilt*. In his view, at this stage, the infantile ego, which is weak and unintegrated, has to cope with, and control the power of, the id and its products. At this time, the infant will experience a certain quality of anxiety, "a crude fear" (e.g., "Have I eaten the mother?"). The infant's introjects are sub-human and primitive, and the dependence on the object is absolute. At this earliest ego stage, the infant cannot experience "guilt", because the ego is insufficiently strong, organized, and integrated.[16]

It follows that the development of a capacity for guilt, logically and experientially, requires a degree of emotional growth and a certain ego health, as well as what Winnicott refers to as "hope". For this maturation to occur, there must be a "facilitating environment", by which he means a mothering figure to care for, hold, and manage, the infant (Winnicott, 1963, p. 75). He further develops this idea of a "natural" but complex process of "holding" and "good-enough mothering", by distinguishing the "object mother" from the "environmental mother" (*ibid.*, p. 79). On the infant's side of the story, he describes the achievement of a "capacity for concern" and a capacity to "use" the object. The object mother's task is to be "reliably present" for the infant, and to survive (in phantasy and in reality) the damaging attacks. As Winnicott puts it, she must "survive the instinct driven episodes" (*ibid.*, p. 76). On the other hand, the environment mother must also be available to provide love, care, management, reliability etc., and all that is implied in Winnicott's central idea of "holding". In his words, she must be able to "accept the restitutative gesture". Finally as development proceeds, both aspects of the mothering figure have to be available for "use" by the infant.

> The object is *in phantasy* always being destroyed. This quality of "always being destroyed" makes the reality of the surviving object felt as such,strengthens the feeling tone, and contributes to object-constancy. The object can now be used. [Winnicott, 1971b, p. 93, original italics]

How, then, for Winnicott, does a mature and healthy superego come to be achieved by the infant? He describes this as a gradual process in which a "capacity for concern" is developed between the ages of five to six months and two years. This theoretical formulation is clearly based on Klein's formulation of "the depressive position", in which the infant has become capable of tolerating ambivalence (i.e., bringing together its love and hate) and directing these affects towards the mothering-figure, held in the mind as a whole person. However, in Winnicott's terms, it is when the object mother and the environment mother come together in the infant's mind that reparation and mending become a possibility.

In health, this developmental process involves the infant's intro-jection of a pre-oedipal, maternal superego that is closely connected with the capacity for concern. At this new stage of growth, the infant can now hold, and tolerate, conflict resulting from ambivalence. Winnicott describes how, in developing a sense of guilt, the infant's ego has "employed certain controlling forces", which he identifies as the "superego". In arriving at his own formulation, he acknow-ledges Freud's original concept of the "superego", and accepts Klein's revision of the theory, with its emphasis on the pre-oedipal sources, the mother's role in its formation, and the contribution of the infant's early phantasies. However, in contrast to Klein, he gives more emphasis to the role and significance of the actual, care-taking mother.

It is when the infant begins to emerge from the stage of absolute dependence on the mother's "holding", and can begin to "hold" its own anxiety, that the crude affect alters in quality and becomes "a sense of guilt". When this conflict can be held, and tolerated, by the infant, the anxiety gradually matures into guilt (Winnicott, 1958, p. 18).

According to Winnicott, in health, an "innate morality" gradu-ally develops. In a benign and mature development of the individ-ual person, there occurs an increasing ego strength and control of id drives, accompanied by an ability to take personal responsibility for actions, and by a capacity for remorse and reparation. In the wider social context, which was always in the background of Winnicott's deliberations, he regarded the development of a *true morality* as a "fundamental constructive element in play and work". The mature superego always implies, for him, an ability to compromise, and to accept as part of the self the "mores of local society" (Davis & Wallbridge, 1981, pp. 72–76).

He also writes at length about *false morality*, problems in the development of a sense of guilt, and abnormalities in superego formation, citing and illustrating the abnormal sense of guilt found in cases of obsessional neurosis, and in melancholia. In both these illnesses, hate has become more powerful than love, and an over-whelming sense of guilt paralyses the individual. An internalized morality that is false to the self (i.e., based on the compliance of the false-self) hinders the individual's maturity and personal growth. (See the epigraph to Chapter Three, in which Winnicott implies that the struggle to feel "real" may be inhibited or even defeated.)

The immature, inoperative, or absent superego is associated with various forms of loss or absence. These include the capacity for concern, the sense of responsibility, a sense of guilt, a reparative capacity, and a personal integrity. In the development of the super-ego, the absence of a reparative capacity as an aspect of guilt may be particularly serious, since Winnicott emphasizes that what is missing is the drive towards "constructive or actively loving behaviour . . . reviving the object, making the object better again, rebuilding the damaged thing . . ." (Winnicott, 1963, p. 103).

In drawing this chapter to a conclusion, I wish to mention Michael Balint's work. Although he makes few references to super-ego theory, his comments on a superego role in psychoanalytic education and training are particularly interesting (Stewart, 1996).

Balint's concern was with the negative role of the superego in the organization of training in psychoanalytic institutes. He points to the danger of a dogmatic attitude in training analysts, which he considers can produce a too respectful and compliant attitude in candidates. He also criticizes what he describes as "primitive initiation ceremonies", which act to produce strongly established and lasting identifications with the analyst. In Balint's view, these identifications can result in the development of an over-strong superego in the candidate, and a consequent weakening of ego functions.

In his discussion, he refers to Sandor Ferenczi's concept of "superego intropression", which denotes a certain type of educative process in which "a rule or precept is forced into the superego". Balint points out that such a process may lead psychoanalysts to over-emphasize "small group differences", and minimize or hide "the essential agreements".[17]

Other contributions to superego theory

James Strachey was among the first British analysts who, much influenced by Klein and influencing her followers, drew attention to *the savage superego* in the child. In a classical and influential paper published in 1934, he argued that this superego had been "swallowed" into the ego by introjection and that, once there, it was unable to be tolerated. It was therefore again projected and then introjected, a process which created "an even more severe super-ego" which, in a vicious circle, was then again projected. As a result of this process, the ego became dominated by an "implacable super-ego", and Strachey concluded that this constituted "the neurotic predicament" (Strachey, 1934).

To combat this situation, Strachey suggested that the analyst in role was experienced as tolerating the patient's free associations, and came to act as a more benign and kindly *auxiliary superego*. In his view, although the superego reasserted itself and its malign effect on the ego, the analytic process, in time, was therapeutic because the transference insured that libidinous and hostile impulses were now directed towards the analyst and away from the patient's superego. It followed, for Strachey, that interpretation of the "here and now" transference "in small doses" would become "mutative", because it offered the patient an immediate opportunity to distinguish unconscious phantasy from conscious reality.

Among more recent contributions from analysts working in the Independent tradition is that of Nina Coltart (1992), who gave two interesting introductory public lectures at the British Psychoanalytic Society entitled *The superego, anxiety and guilt* and *Sin and the superego: man and his conscience in society*, and these are now briefly summarized.

The first paper is largely a discussion of the development of Freud's, and post-Freudian, views on the superego. In it, she clarifies and elaborates these ideas in her own refreshing and lively style. Her case examples are particularly illuminating and instructive, and beautifully illustrate the patient's "submissive enslavement" to the superego and its tyrannies, and the consequent "self-inflicted misery" that it demands. However, she also adds to these attacks on the self some of the positive aspects, and benign functions, of the superego. She describes "its smiling face" and lists its beneficial functions as ". . . self observation, self-reflection, kindly criticism . . . appreciation, esteem and love".

In the second paper, Coltart, following in Freud's footsteps, discusses the relevance of the superego for the study of the community, and the individual in society. She points out how this topic does, to some extent, revolve around the central question "What ought I to do ?" This, she observes, is the preoccupation of the more mature mind, which seeks to distinguish "right" from "wrong". She suggests that, in all cultures, *conscience* has evolved as a concept to help provide an answer to this question. She concludes that, because of the centrality of "conflict" in the human situation, any answer is bound to be ambiguous and, to that extent, partial and limited.[18]

Following a thorough, comprehensive exploration of psychoanalysis and the human condition, Coltart concludes that Freud insisted on:

> the fundamental intractability of the human condition and the nature of mind, as redefining and sustaining the tough authenticity of human existence that formerly had been ratified only by God ... [his work also offers] a coherent attempt to bring sense, weight, and meaning to the eternal factors in human life i.e. guilt, anxiety, suffering, sin and the superego. [1992, pp. 76, 78]

In drawing this chapter to a close, I wish to mention the monumental research published as *The Freud–Klein Controversies, 1941–1945*, edited by Pearl King and Ricardo Steiner, which indexes over fifty references to the superego. These describe interesting and important debates on such topics as the development and dating of the superego, its genesis, formation, and introjection, its stages, and its relationship with guilt and identification.

Among therapists working within an Independent orientation, Berkowitz (1999, p. 118) has drawn attention to "superego anxieties" in both patient and analyst, and Rosenberg (1999), in an exploration of the erotic transference, has described how, when erotic feelings are unacceptable to the superego, they are kept within the limbo of repression. She also points out how: "if the superego is not overwhelming, it is possible for the patient to disclose and explore love pangs [and] ... accompanying feelings of jealousy and exclusion and eventually to become aware of the therapist's genuine interest and acceptance" (Rosenberg, 1999, pp. 140–141).

Most recently, Ann Horne, a child and adolescent psychoanalytic psychoanalyst, has discussed the principles and practice of supervision. In her view, there is no "correct" psychoanalytic technique which can be applied indiscriminately to patients. She favours, instead, the idea of a set of "principles" that require (sometimes "playful") adaptation, both to the individual case and in the supervisory situation. She describes the image of the child psychotherapist in the guise of a *harsh, professional superego* that lurks over the patient's shoulder, like a "Great Child Pychotherapist in the Sky". She offers an illustration of a seriously abused and neglected child, "Kelly", in which the therapist became so "caught up" with her own superego, and countertransference, that she became unable to think. This was also a case in which this image of the therapist as a fierce God "dominated the mental life" and, in Horne's view, required her *not* to offer interpretations that mirrored the girl's punitive superego. In general, she writes in favour of an approach which "tempers" the superego and leads the patient to internalize the "more affective attitudes" of the therapist (Horne, 2006, pp. 230–231).

Horne also challenges, as unrelated to the "reality" of practice, a type of rigidly defined, professional *ego ideal*, which assumes an image of the "correct" child psychotherapist, who is pictured sitting in the therapy room, "calmly" gathering in "all aspects of the child's problems and behaviour into one succinct mutative inter-pretation—the all encompassing comment that changes the way the child makes sense of himself" (*ibid.*, p. 225).

In this discussion of the superego's relation to the internal object, I have considered various post-Freudian viewpoints, mainly derived from analysts and therapists working in the British psycho-analytic tradition. These contributions have been selected, in each case, as making a valuable addition to superego theory and, by implication, to analytic practice. In the next chapter, I will consider some of the very serious effects that can occur when superego guilt and a capacity for concern are absent in the individual, and/or the group, and when the external object may be attacked and destroyed.

Notes

1. In the light of this limitation, I wish to acknowledge the important contributions to superego theory of many other analysts working worldwide. Among these colleagues are: Arlow, Mahler, Jacobson, Modell, Kernberg, Loewald, Blum, and Ogden in the USA. For other

work in the area of object relations, see Buckley (1986) and Etchegoyen (1991), who cites important contributions from South America.

2. Holder quotes Anna Freud: "... identification with them [parents] is accomplished only gradually and piecemeal. Even though the super-ego already exists ... its dependence on the objects to which it owes its existence must not be overlooked" (p. 82).

3. In a discussion of puberty, Anna Freud (1958) writes:

> ... there is often evidence of a transient attempt to effect a hypercathexis of all the contents of the superego. This is proba-bly the explanation of ... the idealism ... asceticism ... [and] leads to the rupture of the relation with the superego and so renders inoperative the defensive measures prompted by super-ego anxiety [the result is that] ... the ego is ... violently thrown back ... to ... primitive protective mechanisms.

4. The suggestion of an "extra analytic" dimension in the theory and prac-tice of child analysis has given rise to controversy, and is subject to misunderstanding among child analysts of different orientations. For clarification, see especially Holder (2005, p. 90) and Hurry (1998, p. 34).

5. In what follows, I am greatly indebted to Holder (2005) for my summary of his comprehensive account, which compares the work of Anna Freud and Melanie Klein.

6. For a critique of Klein's theories, see Spitz and Kris, cited by Holder.

7. The features associated with the psychotic part of the personality were an over-endowment of destructive impulses, and a violent hatred of internal and external reality, and of all healthy internal and external relationships connected with "linking".

8. In her comprehensive survey of post-Kleinian research, Bott-Spillius (1988) includes other important papers on pathological organizations that are particularly relevant to the exploration of the cruel and sadis-tic superego.

9. O'Shaughnessy (1999) describes a patient, Mr B, in "a more fluctuating transference situation". In the initial phase of the analysis with this patient, there was "a void" because he was unable to link with others. She describes a "developmental impasse", which was illustrated in the patient's "studied response to interpretations", by means of which he "unlinked" his connection with the analyst. However, in a later phase (three years afterwards), he showed signs of improvement (e.g., shar-ing dreams). She vividly describes the patient's psychic predicament as a result of his pathological "Super" ego.

10. See Riesenberg-Malcolm's (1999) discussion of the superego. Britton refers with approval to Mrs Malcolm's view that disturbing internal objects can "remain conscious throughout life", and may affect a person in "unfavourable circumstances". However, he questions her view that all internal objects operate as the superego (Britton, 2003, p. 74).

11. See also Fairbairn's *Selected Papers* in Fairbairn-Birtles and Scharff (1994, pp. 80–115).

12. Coltart (1992), in a chapter on the superego, observes that Freud himself was the first to propose the idea that separation, in its manifold forms, is the deepest form of anxiety.

13. The earliest stage is of "infantile dependence", in which the dependence is total, and centred on "being given to" and the satisfaction of basic needs. The part object has a significant role (the mouth = libidinal organ, the breast = libidinal object), and the "other" is known only as an aspect of the self (i.e., primary identification). The carer is bound to fail at this stage, since no provision is made for her own needs (Fairbairn, 1946, p. 145).

14. At this period, the infant has begun to realize that the "other" is not the same as him or her, and a separation process is initiated. External objects are now treated as inner objects by the infant, who projects the "rejecting" or "exciting" objects on to others in the environment, and relates to them in those terms.

15. Maturity is relative, and implies, for Fairbairn, the capacity to give. At this stage, there is an avoidance of the excessive splitting, projection, and repression, of the schizoid position, and, to achieve it, is for him the aim of the therapeutic encounter.

16. At the earliest stage the "other" is viewed as part of the self. This libidinal dependence is expressed through the attitude of "taking" from the object (i.e.. feeding from and receiving love). However, strictly speaking there is not yet an "I" in the statement "Have *I* eaten the mother?"

17. In his last (1954) paper on training (reprinted as a chapter in *Primary Love and Psychoanalytic Technique*, 1965), Balint refers to the possibility of the "contamination" of the training analysis by "power politics" and the "taboo of idealisation", which he says may inhibit in the candidate "*the full brunt of fierce* aggressiveness" (my italics). This process, he suggests, may have a kind of inverse negative effect on members of analytic societies in which pent up aggression may be displaced on to outsider critics (quoted by Stewart, 1996, p. 66).

18. In her wide-ranging and erudite discussion of the concept of "sin", Coltart relates some of Freud's ideas on the superego to the Judaic-

Christian tradition, Buddhism, the Bible, Greek philosophy, tragedy, and other texts.

5.10.

CHAPTER FIVE

Pathology, splitting, and fragmentation in the system: the superego, the object and the Holocaust[1]

"God has done an uneven piece of work, for a large majority of men have brought along with them only a modest amount of it [i.e., the individual conscience] or scarcely enough to be worth mentioning"

(Freud, 1933a[1932], "The dissection of the psychical personality", p. 61)

"I was like a man following a trail of bloodstained footprints through the snow without realising someone has been injured . . .

He was always a man not only of many parts but divided in himself"

(Sereny, 1995)[2]

As I have previously shown, a description of the system superego necessarily includes the functions of "self-obser-vation, conscience and . . . the ideal", together with such aspects of the mind as a conscious and unconscious sense of guilt,

the capacity for concern, the capacity for remorse, a sense of morality, ethical standards, and so on. In earlier chapters, I have also
described and illustrated Freud's account of how, in such pathological states as obsessional neurosis and melancholia, this system
has a tendency to turn inwards and attack the self.

In this chapter, I consider some consequences that result when
superego hostility is turned outwards against the object. In particular, I will discuss how such powerful aggression, when directed at
the object, may give rise in the subject to primitive ego defences
such as splitting, projection, and projective identification.

I use the example of the Holocaust to illustrate how a sustained,
murderous activity was directed against a detested object, with the
final aim of annihilation. In what follows, I use the term
"Holocaust" to refer to the mass extermination in the Second World
War of many millions of men, women, and children, mainly Jews,
but also including gypsies, mentally handicapped persons in
Germany, homosexual persons, Russian and Polish prisoners of
war, and other "undesirables" comprising many nationalities. This
mass killing, initiated by the Nazi leaders, was carried out by
members of the infamous SS, the Gestapo, the German army, and
many others who were allied with Nazi Germany.

This deliberate murder of millions of people was also carried
out with the utmost cruelty and sadism that was superordinary in
its management and dedication. I suggest that the scale of system-
atized killing implies a corruption of the superego systems, in
group and individual (i.e., a reversal of normal civilized values),
that was unique.

However, in this discussion, I also assume that an historical
event of this dimension will not yield easily to a psychoanalytic, or
any other single explanation, and I am not proposing a reductive
and simplistic approach of this kind. I seek rather to raise some
questions that relate to how the ordinary human constraints on the
practice of cruelty (i.e., conscience, guilt, concern, moral responsibility, etc.), which have been examined in this book, could be so
undeveloped, or become so seriously damaged, as to be (or appear
to have been) virtually absent in the perpetrators of the Holocaust.

I have earlier suggested that the concept of the ego ideal is of
central importance to the process by which a group of persons come
to submit their personal will to the will of an admired leader, by a

process of substitution. Each individual in question may, thereby, come to adopt the attitudes of the leader and the group, which may in turn be linked to certain cultural or racial prejudices (Freud, 1921c).

It has been observed that, in this process, such persons find satisfaction in maintaining a strategy for initiating, and preserving, their narcissistic illusions, by means of the new authority of the group. By this means, they attempt a union of ego and ideal in which the individual superego becomes submerged.

The Nazi ego ideal and "morality"

In the case of the Nazis, the worship of such an ideal was twofold. On the one hand, there was the worship of the all-powerful mother-goddess of early mythology, and the worship of the "heroes" who died in her service. This ideology proposed a return to nature (*Blut und Boden*) by means of which the individual achieved the illusion of omnipotence by a merging with the mother. In this sense, Hitler was able to activate the primitive wish for the fusion of ego with ideal (Chasseguet-Smirgel, 1975).[3]

On the other hand, it appears that Hitler also achieved his dictatorial status as *Führer*, and father-figure of the Nazi take-over. As an illustration of this fanatical and utterly ruthless ideal, centred on the "blood" philosophy, consider a comment from another of Hitler's close associates in the Nazi hierarchy, Heinrich Himmler, who is said to have once remarked:

> We must be honest, decent, loyal, and comradely to members of our own blood, but to nobody else. . . . If 10,000 Russian females fall down from exhaustion digging an anti-tank ditch . . . That interests me only in so far as the anti-tank ditch for Germany is finished. [Quoted by Lifton & Markusen, 1988, p. 194]

The way in which such a perverse ego ideal can become "blind" to reality is illustrated by the fanatical war of extermination waged against the Jews. For the Nazis, this project became a separate "war" in which resources (e.g., transport) were diverted from the primary war effort, which was fought against the allied forces. In this fanatical blindness, a process can be observed that involved a complex splitting mechanism between extremes of "them" (ideally bad) and "us" (ideally good) . For the Nazis, the Jews had come to personify both weakness and power. The Jews were not only despised as weak and inferior, but it was widely believed that they were child murderers, and that they also planned to financially control and take over the world. Thus, the weakness of the host nation, Germany, (which had resulted from defeat in the First World War) was projected upon the Jews. However, their fantasized power (i.e., "the chosen people") was a basis for identification with them (i.e., in the sense that the "Aryan" race came to be idealized).

A further illustration of this splitting process is illustrated by the fact that the extreme cruelty that took place was also often practised by "ordinary" people, who were, it appears, able without difficulty to set aside the usual considerations of conscience. Such murderous behaviour was, then, not restricted to the murderous and sadistic acts of typical criminals and psychopaths. There is also much evidence that many of the unspeakable actions that were performed were not simply part of the military process of "obeying orders" (as claimed, for example, by the defence at the Nuremberg trials), but were carried out on individual initiative, and often with passionate dedication and zeal. Also, with few exceptions, the perpetrators did not express dissent or refuse to participate. It may be concluded from this observation, that the idea of the "ordinary" or "normal" superego system is complex, and echoes Freud's description of the weakness and vulnerability of the system, which was quoted in the epigraph to this chapter. It is also interesting that some perpetrators made claims, backed up by an extraordinary degree of rationalization, that they were *not without conscience*.[4, 5]

Attempts have nevertheless been made, by research workers, to link such fanatical cruelty and sadism to a "specific character structure", and one that itself may be associated with extreme degrees of splitting and dissociation. This pattern of behaviour has been referred to as *Kadavergehorsam*, which is usually translated as *blind obedience* (but is literally "obedience unto death"). However, the German word can also be understood in the sense of behaviour that exhibits a corpse-like or robotic manner, which implies a person who acts without will and, therefore, without conscience.

As is well known, the Nazi ideology was based on Hitler's racial theory, which can be summarized as follows: People were divided into the racially "pure" and racially "impure" categories, and the former were subdivided into those on a "high" plain and those on a "low" plain. The "Aryans" belonged to the most superior race and the Jews to the most inferior, with the implication that the Aryan had nothing but good qualities and the Jew had nothing but bad. Part of this argument was that the "bad" Jew also had designs on the "good" blood of the Aryan.[6, 7]

For example, it was from this viewpoint that the members of the SS were selected because of their "Nordic" blood and the qualities that were considered to spring from it. Among these qualities was the capacity for absolute loyalty and obedience. I shall consider this sub-group of perpetrators, from the point of view of the superego concept.[8]

This Nazi philosophy, when carried to its ultimate conclusion (especially the "pure" blood theory), resulted in the genocide of millions of the "impure". The members of the SS regarded this genocide as a necessary cleansing activity and, in that sense, a "normal" and praiseworthy act.[9]

However, there is evidence that some of its members acted to obtain gratification of their murderously aggressive drives by over-riding the conflict caused by a disapproving "conscience". In these cases, and due to a variety of factors (e.g., projection of guilt, ratio-nalization, and transforming the meaning of the murderous act), it is as if the "normal superego" may have been operative, but its curbing influence on the murderous impulse was clearly ineffec-tive. These SS perpetrators were, therefore, only identified *in part* with their own murderous activities.

A second sub-group of SS personnel (and perhaps the majority) appeared to have developed a more abnormal (i.e., "criminal") superego, in the sense of becoming easily identified with a criminal morality (a criminal ideal), and the members of this group were wholly identified with their own acts. From 1933 onwards, the Nazis developed a "hate morality" (backed by later legal measures), which depended on the idea of superior and inferior races, and the hatred was widely and intensively disseminated in schools, colleges, the Hitler Youth, radio, films, newspapers, and books.

Those who joined the SS, therefore, chose to implement the morality they had been taught as correct by the standards of their own society. In many cases, a "normal enough", civilized, and humane superego seems to have been totally, or partially, replaced by a corrupt and perverse ("criminal") superego in the service of a tribal ego ideal.[10]

Questions remain, however, as to how, and why, such a transformation can take place. Several factors acting together would seem to throw light on this issue. The majority of persons tend to "follow the crowd" (especially when they also engage in "follow my leader"), and easily accept the values of the society that they are part of. Since, as Freud observed, the "normal" superego is relatively weak, unstable, and unreliable, it requires continuous reinforcement by such binding influences as the law, political philosophy, religion, and ethics. When such influences are weakened, or replaced by malign ideas, the system superego becomes weaker and more vulnerable. In some individuals, a "general immaturity", accompanied by a high suggestibility, has also been noted. Such factors, however, clearly do not get to the root of the problem. Compare Cohen's (1988) description of what he calls the "abyss of bestialities" and the "cool calculating manner" in which the misery of the victims was inflicted.

Another feature in vulnerable personalities of this kind is that of weak ego development. This may have been influenced by the crushing in the 1930s of the more healthy educational, social, and democratic, forces in German society. For example, in the Nazi organizations concerned, any "deviant member" tended to be expelled, or even sometimes liquidated. In the SS, the aim of such elimination was to reinforce group cohesion (referred to as *Blutkitt*, translated as "blood cement").[11]

The quality of child rearing practice (i.e., authoritarian, rigid, punitive parental attitudes) has also been emphasized as a contributory factor in this process.

One focus of research into the genocidal and murderous attitude of the perpetrators has been on a sample of medically qualified members of the SS. The doctors who were involved in the killing process in the camps were either directly active, or were passive perpetrators. In the latter case, it is well established that the neglect of the medical and hygienic care of the prisoners resulted in a vastly increased mortality. The active process of selection for extermination, in Auschwitz, was carried out exclusively by SS doctors. In one example, a doctor called Dr Konig is reported as *being tortured* by this selection activity, and as having to drink alcohol excessively to carry it out. The author notes that "something of Dr Konig's former superego had remained alive, which he could silence by means of alcohol" (Cohen, 1988, p. 263).

In other camp situations, non-Jewish prisoners who had shown signs of illness were often selected by the doctors to be murdered. In Buchenwald camp, the doctors were also active in the selection of prisoners for medical experiments, and there is little evidence that those involved ever made any formal protest. In fact, it seems that many members of the German medical profession exhibited a willingness to use their medical power to abuse many defenceless victims who had been stripped of their rights to normal care. What is striking about this situation is the lack of the *normal conscience*, and of medical ethics, displayed by the physicians in question.[12]

In an attempt to throw light on this behaviour, Eli Cohen reports that, as early as 1935, German doctors had been instructed in the ideals of National Socialism, e.g., "[that] love of one's fellow men had to disappear, especially in regard to inferior and a-social elements . . . in order to secure the continuance of a racially pure people free from hereditary taint for all eternity" (Gutt, 1935, cited by Cohen, 1988, p. 266).

More recent research into the motivation, and superego pathology, of the Nazi doctors has thrown further light on the general breakdown in medical ethics and the display of individual criminality. The ideal Nazi doctor was not supposed to have a conscience and, therefore, was not supposed to worry about his ultimate responsibility in the killing process. Even those who may have, at first, opposed murderous experiments on the helpless prisoners later acted in a criminal fashion, with such rationalization that "orders" from superiors had to be obeyed and that, in any case, they acted for the "general good". What is clear is that doctors involved gradually became progressively brutalized.

Those who had a normally functioning superego system may have managed to come to terms with its protests by defences that have been variously described as "psychic numbing", "doubling", and "dissociation". These defences are linked with the perpetrators' unconscious attempts at self-protection from the effects of their actions on others, and specifically from the kind of brutality demanded in the mass killing of human beings.

"Psychic numbing" is described as "a form of dissociation characterised by the diminished capacity or inclination to feel and usually includes separation of thought from feeling". "Doubling" is another dissociative mental state that largely takes place outside of awareness. In this process, the individual comes to develop a fragmented "second" self, which tends to act independently. It is as if a second self has separated out from the "prior self". Thus, the SS doctors developed an "Auschwitz self" that participated in the murders, while the prior self was maintained as an "off-duty self" and was demonstrated in a kindly attitude to (their own) children and to animals. (For a detailed commentary of this research, see Lifton, 1986, 1993; Lifton & Markusen, 1988.)

The doubling which led to the formation of the Auschwitz self involved the internalization in the doctor of the "norms" of the Auschwitz environment. This has been described as:

> the reversals of healing and killing, the operative Nazi biomedical vision, the extreme numbing that rendered killing no longer killing, struggles with omnipotence (deciding who would live or die) and impotence (being a cog in a powerful machine) maintaining a medical identity while killing and somehow finding meaning in the environment. [Lifton & Markusen, 1988, p. 106]

One doctor commented that "killing" had become part of "the Auschwitz weather" (*ibid.*, p. 107).

I turn now from the discussion of the murderous attack on the object, and its splitting effects on the perpetrator's superego system, to a second focus of research, i.e., the effects on the superego system of the survivor and his/her children.

The Holocaust victims and fragmentation of the superego

The evidence arising from the testament of survivors of the Nazi concentration camps suggests that many inmates were often reduced to behaving like starving animals. In some instances, the conflict that resulted from the situation was powerful enough to fragment the superego. It has been suggested that, in the horrendous, hostile environment that the victims were forced to endure, there was probably the intrusive, subconscious thought that the death of one's neighbour would satisfy the perpetrator's lust to kill, at least on a temporary basis, so that a person's own existence was therefore prolonged for at least one more day.

It was as if such personal survival often demanded a temporary suspension of superego function, which then led to a regression to the early and primitive developmental stage that has been previously described. Such regressive states were to have serious aftereffects for the survivors. In some cases, the price paid for this overwhelming of the superego system, and the perpetration of acts against the most firmly established taboos, contributed after the war to a permanent psychotic state of depression in some survivors (Krell & Sherman, 1997).

However, even under extremely hostile conditions, the victims reacted in different ways and how they did so throws light on the complexity of the superego. For example, in research with children who were imprisoned and who suffered greatly in the camps, it has been found that many were more outspoken than adults, that they joined a resistance movement, and sought out ways to feed their families. It is also reported that some even "gained strength and a new zest for life" (Kestenberg, 1993).

One remarkable case of exceptional behaviour in the camps is exemplified in the story of two adolescent survivors of Auschwitz, Helmuth and Harry, who were reunited fifty years after the war, when their story was reported in the press. The episode in the camp took place when Helmuth, a thirteen-year-old Jewish boy, naked and starving, was lining up for inspection by the infamous Nazi doctor, Joseph Mengele, who waved him to the left (i.e., condemned him to die).

The following astonishing sequence of events then took place. Helmuth confronted Mengele and begged for his life. In his own words, he walked up to Mengele and clicked his heels, in an imitation of the Hitler Youth. He spoke perfect "Hochdeutsch" in the Berlin manner, and this appeared to impress Mengele, who "gave him back" his life and, in addition, offered him a job as a messenger. Helmuth now marched away, but was then approached by another inmate, Harry, who asked him to beg for his life. Helmuth did so, but Mengele now lost his temper, and told the boys he would spare only one life and that they had to draw straws to see who this was to be. Harry lost, but urged Helmuth to make a third plea. This time Mengele agreed, perhaps impressed by Helmuth's extreme bravery or perhaps for reasons of his own.

Helmuth, aged sixty-seven at the time of the reunion, reflected on this extraordinary courageous and altruistic behaviour in relation to "the object" (a stranger). He said, "Maybe I hypnotized Mengele. Maybe for one moment I made him think differently of the Jews. He must have had some respect for the thirteen-year-old who gambled his life to look after his friend."

The full newspaper report of the episode of Helmuth and Harry clearly demonstrates the vicissitudes, the ebb and flow, of the superego system, as observed in a particular situation in which there was an extreme danger to life. In the rest of the story, which is summarized below, one can observe the power of splitting, and the shifts to and fro, among various aspects of the superego system (i.e., the ego ideal, the superego, the sense of guilt, and conscience and the capacity for concern).

Both boys became servants to the SS officers, but their continuing survival appears to have depended on a dramatic splitting process, in which they were forced to live a kind of double life. In the daytime, they were given bright uniforms to wear but, at night, they were forced to sleep six to a bunk with the other prisoners. Harry's task was to raise and lower the banner, *"Arbeit macht frei"*, and Helmuth, among other things, cleaned motorbikes. What becomes clear was that their lives were lived on a knife-edge and that they continually experienced terrible things. Harry, for example, was constantly threatened with a gun. When operations were performed in the camp on unfortunate inmates without anaesthetic, they heard agonized screams. In their account of their time spent in the camp, they remembered the omnipresent "stench of smoke" that filled the air. In order to survive, however, the boys were forced to turn in on themselves. This process involved an unavoidable and poignant split, and an identification with the aggressor, which is exemplified in a comment by Helmuth :

> In the evenings, I would break down and cry and think of my family but at 3.30 in the morning I was cold and self-contained, as invincible as the officers. The people who had died overnight were dragged outside and you stepped over their bodies.

At other times, an empathic, compassionate, and even "fighting back" attitude was re-established, in that both boys gave scraps of food to the other prisoners, and Helmuth provided glass bottles to make bombs to blow-up a gas chamber (*The Sunday Times*, 4 May, 1997).

I turn next to consider some of the long-term after-effects of the Holocaust experience on the superego systems of survivors and their children.

Transmission, transposition, and the superego

In general, the destruction of ordinary standards of living, care, and concern, in the camps led to serious fragmentation of the superego that continued to have persistent effects long after the war, in the form of painful mental states and bodily disorders. However, research suggests that even the long-term psychopathological effects were not necessarily irreversible. With the passage of time and the healing process, it was possible in some, especially child, survivors for the old, normal values to be re-established, and for the superego system to be reconstructed and reintegrated. Kestenberg and Brenner (1996) write:

> As former child survivors regained as adults a feeling of worth and could re-establish their old values and *re-build their superegos*, their children were greatly helped in integrating their own. Parenthood raised the survivors' aspirations and helped them *to heal the rift in the superego*. [p. 67, my italics]

I turn next to discuss some of the long-term after-effects. It has been established that many survivors continued to suffer from "death imprints" (i.e., intrusive images that had become embedded in their minds) and other serious life problems, long after the war ended. It was these after-(and long-term) effects that were frequently unconsciously transmitted to the second generation, and were linked to a malfunctioning in the ego and superego systems of that generation (Bergmann & Yucovi, 1982; Karpf, 1996; Kestenberg, 1993; Kogan, 1995; Pines, 1993; Wardi, 1992).

For example, there are many reports of second generation children growing up with a conscious awareness of the hovering presence of death in their own lives. Dina Wardi (1992) has described how certain children in a survivor family may have been unconsciously selected and become "memorial candles", a process that may take place both in homage to the loss of close relatives and, more generally, to the murdered millions.

One study of effects on the second generation has focused specifically on the superego system. It starts from the observation that, in the camps, the very core of this system in the victims was systematically attacked, and demolished, by the conditions of living. This was, as it were, often the price of survival. Later, after the war, with the birth of a new generation, it was found that two major unconscious phantasies of the survivors came to be transmitted to the children. The first was an invitation for the second generation child to act as a replacement for a child that had been lost in the camps (a profound and moving dramatization of such effects is illustrated in the film, *Left Luggage*).[13]

The second, and related, phantasy was the unconscious wish that the second-generation child would carry out a special mission in his or her own life. This task involved a personal achievement that would have the powerfully desired effect of healing past injuries. The author reports that, as the second-generation children are drawn into the survivor's psychic reality, "superego and ego ideal elements constitute a central organising principle of their involvement in parental re-adaptation" (Bergmann, 1982, p. 289).

This situation then becomes potentially pathological, because it interferes with the child's self-representation and the autonomy of the child's normally developing superego and ego ideal. The ensuing conflict is one between the child's superego and the parents' ego ideal. The author concludes that, if this conflict cannot be resolved, a lasting hostile bond may develop in which the child's superego becomes trapped in the attempt to fulfil the child's perception of insatiable parental needs (*ibid.*, pp. 287–309).

One recent account of the experience of growing up in a survivor family, an outstanding account for its insights, has been provided by the journalist, and writer, Anne Karpf (1996). Her testimony is especially valuable because, as a result of her therapeutic experience, she was able to monitor changes in her "self" and superego systems.

Karpf describes how she adopted various kinds of compulsive behaviour, as a means of keeping a vaguely sensed "death threat" at bay. In her fantasy life, the Second World War was fought over again with the "self" as the battleground. Her experience included an intensive urge to repair the damage to the parents and a compulsive drive to achieve, in relation to unconscious family demands. For her, as for her parents, achievement had become equated with survival.

She describes the experience of her parents as rather like fragile china that had been broken and then repaired, with herself as the "glue". This experience seemed to particularly affect the normal developmental task of separation, a process that was filled with pain and guilt, and which implied parental breakdown. When a separation was, to some extent, achieved, the death-centred thoughts returned. She writes movingly, ". . . at the age of twenty-five and with the encouragement of my mother, I did leave home . . . but phoned home every day to check that they were still alive" (Karpf, 1996, p. 54).

In my own experience of working with groups of second-generation survivors, some (especially female) members of the group have related an almost identical story. It seems clear that, for Karpf, as for her parents, separation was equivalent to rupture, and any ending was very dangerous. This seemed to arise because there was no trust in reunion (see also the case material I describe below on the question of loss of trust). Karpf writes movingly of the transmission process: "My parents . . . [had experienced] sudden fractures . . . [and] *their experience had become my own.* I soaked up their fear of loss. For all of us separation had become symbolically equivalent of death" (*ibid.*, p. 44, my italics).

It is as if, in this example, Karpf's identification with her mother were *total.* The normal development of the ego ideal (i.e., the internalization of parental values and standards), central to the development of the whole superego system, had, in her case, become grossly distorted in the direction of over-compensation and over-concern. She writes, for example, that she would have gladly become one with her parents and suffered for them, but that this, even if realized, could still never have matched their suffering. Such over-identification of this kind in the second generation also seems to involve direct transmission into the body, and her account provides harrowing descriptions of various life-long psychosomatic disorders. (See also Kogan, 1995; Pines, 1993.)

Other researchers into second-generation experience have pointed to a fantasy process of "bringing the dead back to life". The process of transposition has been described as like descending into a "time tunnel" (i.e., living in two worlds at the same time). Living in the parental world includes primitive phantasies of rescue, and of restoring the dead of the previous generation. This "living in the past and the present" also implies an accompanying split in the superego system (Kestenberg, 1993).

Case material

I have described Karpf's experience and its implications for super-ego development in some detail, not only because it reflects other research accounts of second-generation experience, but also because it provides a comparison with some clinical material of my own, to which I now turn.

Mr A presented as a bright young businessman who sought my help because of a general lack of confidence in relationships, and because of a particular difficulty in separating from his parents.

In what follows, I shall describe how, in the course of therapy, some striking features of his superego system were revealed. These seemed to be connected with the unconscious transmission to him of traumatic effects suffered by his mother, a Holocaust survivor. After about a year in analysis, the patient spoke of a story told to him by his mother, who, when a small child, had been imprisoned in a camp.

In this incident, a guard with a dog had thrown a half-eaten apple in front of the little girl, with the clear intention of setting the dog on the child if she moved. In telling me this, it was clear that my patient's mother had communicated the full emotional impact of the torture and brutality of the guard, and the terror, and her own utter helplessness in the situation.

As we continued to work together on the current dilemmas in his own life, he sometimes returned to this vivid and painful anecdote, which seemed to symbolize current problems in the relationship with his mother. He was intent on both assuming responsibility for keeping his mother "safe" in the present, and on magically "undo-ing" the traumas of the past. In relating how his mother would, when talking to him, bring the past into her present life, he used striking imagery. She would say to him that life was a matter of "dog eats dog" in that, if you did not get the other, they (the other) would get you. He told me how he found this difficult to cope with, because part of him agreed with this viewpoint.

Although Mr A, in his communications to me, revealed that another part of him was more balanced and autonomous, what was most striking was his perception of the external world as essentially dangerous, cruel, and hostile. For example, in one session, he told me of a man who had asked him for money in the street and had then made some hostile remark to him. He, himself, had reacted very strongly to this and had sworn at the man. This incident, he said, had put him in a very bad and fighting mood.

Whatever the actual reality of this story, it seemed to me to illustrate, at least in part, Mr A's projection of the cruel and persecutory internal world that he carried around with him, and which seemed to have had its origins in his mother's past traumatic experience. It was as if he had developed a compulsive need to fight a battle in his present life, in a manner similar to Anne Karpf: one that was not his own. In this way, he was unconsciously attempting to rescue his mother from her sense of helplessness, and himself from his own present helplessness, "to make things better" for her.

Some time later, the patient told me of a time in adolescence when he thought he had become anorexic. At that time, he remembered his experience of school as being "rather like a concentration camp". He related this memory to his current feelings of guilt because of things that he "consumed", and associated this to his mother's experience of starvation in the camp. He said that he felt he could not "consume" because this would be an evil thing. I said that it was as though he also felt himself to be "consumed" by the horrors of the past. He agreed, and related this to his current guilt feelings if he allowed himself to experience even the simplest pleasures in life.

In thinking much later about this material, I understood it differently to mean that he had contributed to the situation that he described by offering himself as a kind of sacrifice, an offer of "self" for his mother to "consume" as a kind of compensation, and it also seemed to me that something similar was going on in the relationship with me. The pull towards merger with his mother and her past was very powerful, and this was reflected in his attitudes to the analyst (e.g., the effect of breaks).

Conclusion

In this chapter I have discussed and tried to illustrate the fundamental processes of splitting and dissociation in the ego and superego systems in both the Nazi perpetrators of genocide and in their
victims. My own clinical material describes a member of the second
generation of Holocaust survivors in whom an undigested parental
ego ideal became connected to an overactive and fragmented superego. My understanding of this material is in general agreement
with the main findings of other analysts and research workers who
have worked with Holocaust survivors and/or their children.

In the case of Mr A, the unconscious intrusion of a parental ego
ideal had resulted in a severe distortion in the patient's capacity for
concern, in the direction of an over-concern; i.e., he carried a heavy
burden of felt responsibility for repairing the effects of the massive
psychic trauma suffered by the parent. This psychopathology had,
in turn, led to distortions in the patient's personal autonomy, and
his sense of self. In my patient's case, what seemed essential was to
help him achieve an intrapsychic act of separation from the internal, persecuting parent. Helped by the analytic process, the patient
was, to a considerable extent, able to achieve a new freedom from
the bond of guilt shared with the traumatized parent.

Notes

1. This chapter is a revised and expanded version of an article previously
   published in Steiner and Johns, 2001.
2. The speaker is Albert Speer, Hitler's architect and Minister of arma-
   ments and war production, sentenced at the Nuremberg trials to twenty
   years' imprisonment for crimes committed under the Nazi regime.
3. Chasseguet-Smirgel has commented that a leader such as Hitler was
   ". . . the promoter of illusion . . . makes it shiver before men's dazzled
   eyes . . . [and is one] who will bring it to fruition". Hitler was, of course,
   greatly aided by Goebbels, the master illusionist, in carrying out this
   task.
4. Storr (1968, p. 97) comments, "Ordinary people have hidden paranoid
   tendencies and a proclivity for brutality. . . . It is a mistake to believe
   that ordinary men are not capable of extremes of cruelty".

5. Browning (1992) quotes a thirty-five year-old metal worker as follows:

> . . . because I reasoned with myself that after all without its mother the child could not live any longer. It was supposed to be, so to speak, *soothing to my conscience to release children unable to be with their mothers.* [p. 73, my italics]

6. See Cohen (1988) for a comprehensive account of Hitler's ideology.
7. Bettleheim writes: "they really believed in a Jewish–Capitalistic world conspiracy against the German people, and that whoever opposed the Nazis participated in it and was therefore to be destroyed" (quoted by Cohen, 1988, p. 237).
8. Rudolf Hoess, the commandant of Auschwitz has commented on the SS law of total obedience as follows:

> Don't you see we SS men were not supposed to think about these things; it never even occurred to us . . . we were all so trained to obey orders without even thinking that the thought of disobeying an order would simply never have occurred to anybody. [Cohen, 1988, p. 258]

9. Hoess commented on his "normality" as follows: "I am entirely normal. Even while I was doing this extermination work, I led a normal family life and so on".
10. Cohen writes:

> Many of these (SS members) had good intelligence . . . benefits of good family life . . . good religious and humane cultural education through the decisive phases of their childhood. Yet [when committing crimes, they] remained completely free from guilt feelings. [1988, p. 233]

Flugel (1945) describes how such a lack of guilt is reinforced by a "supreme sense of moral rightness".

11. See also Martin Gilbert's conclusion, following his interviews with Rudolf Hoess of Auschwitz, where three million people were murdered.

> It was that combination of absolute authoritarianism and hostile racial ideology that had crystallised a new set of social norms in the police state of Nazi Germany and had produced a new species of schizoid, murderous robots, like Colonel Hoess of Auschwitz. [Gilbert, 1950, p. 261]

12. The Hippocratic Oath was abandoned in the training of young doctors who were to staff the infamous euthasania programme that preceded the Holocaust and provided the personnel for the camps.

13. A film produced and directed by Jeroen Krabb in 1998 in Holland. It told the story of how an orthodox Jewish family dealt with the experience of the Holocaust and was based on a short story "Twee Koffers Vol" ("The Shovel and the Loom") by Carl Friedman.

The superego, the self, and morality: contemporary ideas and critical approaches

"There is no such thing as the self . . . that is . . . a finite unique soul or essence that constitutes a person's identity; there is only a subjective position in an infinite web of discourses . . . power, sex, family, science etc."

(David Lodge, 2002, p. 90)[1]

"If the self is a fiction it may perhaps be . . . the greatest achievement of human consciousness, the one that makes us human. . . . The individual self is not a fixed and stable entity, but is constantly being created and modified in consciousness through interaction with others and the world."

(*ibid.*, pp. 16, 91)

In this final chapter, I consider the classical Freudian and some British, post-Freudian psychoanalytic explorations of subjectivity with specific reference to the relations between the ego–self, and the superego. These views will then be discussed in the light of the critique of psychoanalytic (and superego theory) by postmodern thinkers and other commentators. Finally, I shall consider how far, in 2007, the theory of the superego remains a valuable means of insight and understanding in the maintenance and promotion of civilized values and "morality". I begin with a summary of the classical position.

Freud and modernism

Freud's great discoveries and systemization relating to the non-rational, his attempt to investigate and understand mental phenomena, was embedded within the modernist, rational tradition of Western culture. This has been defined as "the literary, historic and philosophical period from 1890 to 1950", a period that is approximately coterminous with the establishment and growth of psychoanalysis (Taylor & Winquist, 2000, p. 251).

The modernist tradition was inspired by the theories, methods, and models of the Enlightenment, which questioned all forms of previous tradition and authority, especially religion and feudalism. Freud was an Enlightenment thinker, who sought to replace fear and superstition with objective truth, and to understand mental life and phenomena by investigation based upon "reason and natural law".

His clinical research and theoretical explorations were rooted in the natural science of his time, especially in its faith in linear "progress" and its claim for the universality of its findings. These aims were allied to modernism, which has been described as:

> the residual belief in the (self-evident) supremacy of logic and scientific rationalism that assumes reality as a whole can be rendered and comprehended, that ideas and concepts are determinate, and that human beings share a level of universal experience with one another that is trans-cultural and trans-historical. [Taylor & Winquist, 2000, p. 251]

In a discussion of the culture of modernism, another observer has commented that Freud 's revolutionary work was a search for "beauty, cleanliness and order" (Bauman, 1993).

Psychoanalytic approaches to the ego–self

In his theoretical approach to "the ego–self", Freud generally refers to *Das Ich* (literally the "I") and avoids the term *Selbst* ("Self"). In his use of *Das Ich*, he did not distinguish between the impersonal ego, a structure of the mental apparatus, and a "self" in the sense of the consciousness of a personal, private "I". However, it seems that the ambiguity contained in this double usage was deliberately not resolved, so that this allowed him to move freely between the objective and the subjective domains (Modell, 1993).

Strachey, in his translation of Freud, also makes no distinction between ego and self, but tended to favour terms such as "ego" and "mental apparatus" as being more scientific and objective. This viewing of the ego from the outside, as it were, is implied in his definition of the ego in *The Ego and the Id* (i.e., "a coherent organization of mental processes"). However, Freud's theory of *Das Ich* must also be considered as a theory of "the self", since it is a structure partly constructed by permanent identifications with "the other" (as, for example, in his famous comment: "Thus the shadow of the object fell upon the ego" (Freud, 1917e, p. 249)).

A feasible theory of the self and subjectivity must, however, also include a perception from the inside, and thereby sustain a link between unconscious process and conscious experience (Modell, 1993).

According to Freud, the human subject is first formed via the central process of repression, in which impulse (i.e., desire) is banished into the unconscious. The root of the Freudian self is, therefore, in the id, and the id can be understood as the seat of desire, in which a totally unconscious, hidden area is constantly pleasure-seeking, in the context of its own special (non-rational) laws.

However, since the self is also connected to the external ("social") world, it follows, according to classical theory, that the development of all human beings involves the negotiation of a necessary shift from unconscious pleasure to external reality. This opposition between pleasure and reality was therefore, for Freud, fundamental to human life.

In classical theory, the infant has also to come to terms with the bodily drives and their accompanying phantasies. The ego–self constantly strives to hold the balance between the unconscious demands for pleasure and the constraints of the internal (superego) and external (social) world. Subjected to the opposing demands of unconscious desire and of external reality, the ego–self becomes

outflanked by them and is, therefore, relatively vulnerable and fragile. Freud has described the ego as "like a man on horseback, who
has to hold in check the superior strength of the horse".

For Freud, the emergence of selfhood is a result of a relationship
to the "other" (the carer), and is formed through a process of identification with this other (see Chapters Two and Three). In this
process, the subject "introjects" the attributes and traits of others,
wholly or in part, and in phantasy form, and transforms them into
the ego–self. The identificatory and introjection process is also
closely connected with feelings of loss, in that the self is partly
constructed in an attempt to become like the lost object:

> . . . an object which was lost has been set up again inside the ego—
> that is an object-cathexis has been replaced by an identification . . .
> this kind of substitution has a great share in determining the
> form taken by the ego and . . . makes an essential contribution [to]
> building . . . "character". [Freud, 1933b, p. 28]

Also, the resolution of the Oedipus complex (the internalization
of the lost object of desire) is the "nodal point" of sexual (and therefore "self") development, and is thus fundamental in the formation
of identity (see Chapters Two and Three).

I turn now to post-Freudian views on the self that arise from the
work of certain British analysts. In these theories, the emphasis was
on the pre-oedipal developmental period, and especially on the
complex emotional internal, and external, links with the mother (or
other primary carer).

These analysts have in common the view that the ego–self is,
from the beginning, in psychological inter-relationship with "the
other". They assume that the internal structuring of the mind is
formed by interpersonal activity and emotional interaction with the
other (see Chapter Four). It follows that the quality (including
socially distorted and destructive elements) of interpersonal relations with the other, and its representations, becomes part of the
actual structure of the self. However, in what follows, I indicate how
they also vary in their theoretical and clinical approaches.

I begin with a summary of Fairbairn's theory of the self. The
concept of dynamic structure as elaborated by Fairbairn is as
follows:

> [The developed psyche is] composed of a multiplicity of dynamic structures falling into two classes (1) ego structures and (2) internal objects . . . [the latter are by a process of introjection] representatives of emotionally significant aspects of persons upon whom the subject depended in early life. [Fairbairn-Birtles & Scharff, 1994]

In Fairbairn's view, the self is built up from internalized object relationships, which themselves transform and structure the unconscious drives. The assumption is that the self has a *primary energy* that initiates object relationships, and its development is closely linked to "primary identification" (i.e., a mode of relatedness at the very earliest stages that implies a total merging between mother and infant). (See Guntrip, 1961, 1968, 1971.)

Since any degree of failure and deprivation will result in frustration for the infant, ego-splitting and pathological compensatory phantasy substitutes (which involve splits and distortions in consciousness) are an inevitable part of the human condition. Such mental pain will, however, increase in relation to the lack of availability and responsiveness in the actual parents.

In his theory, Fairbairn invented the concept of the *anti-libidinal ego*, which had its source in the splitting of the ego in the early months of life, at which time the split-off fragment became unconsciously bonded to the rejecting object. It has been described as "the *anti-wanting I*" (i.e. "that aspect of the self that is contemptuous of neediness", and is, therefore, a much earlier structure than the *classical* superego).

> Rejection [by the maternal object] gives rise to unbearable anger, split off from the central self or ego [i.e., the main part of the self] and disowned by it. [This was originally termed] "the internal saboteur" indicating that in despising rather than acknowledging our libidinal neediness, we insure that we neither get nor seek what we want. The anti-libidinal ego/rejecting object configuration is the cynical, angry self which is too dangerously hostile for us to acknowledge. [Gomez, 1997, pp. 63, 65]

The "badness" of the rejecting object is relocated inside the self, a process that Fairbairn terms *the moral defence*, and this acts to persecute the central self (*ibid.*, p. 65).[2]

For Fairbairn, "the schizoid position", established at the earliest stages of life, structures the self and is the basis for all further personality development. At its most extreme, this mental state results in an individual experience of deadness and futility. Such a state of mind tends to arise when a person's need and anger have been so completely split off and repressed that the core self (i.e., *the central ego/ideal object*) is left empty, and life, and living in relation to others, is without meaning. In this situation, love has become so "bad" and destructive for the subject that other persons become mere adjuncts to the self, at the level of part/self-objects.

Among the object-relations theorists, it is Fairbairn who is the most critical of classical superego theory. As early as 1928, he composed a critique of *The Ego and the Id*, in which he examined the nature of the superego, and charged Freud with an inadequate account of why the superego is unconscious, and of being unclear as to whether or not it is repressed. Fairbairn-Birtles and Scharff give a clear account of Fairbairn's later revised theoretical formulation as follows:

> The need for the child to perceive his parents as "good" leads to a *moral defence* . . . Children define themselves as "bad" in order that their security can be maintained by the "good" parents they construct. That which is felt to be bad in the "self" leads to *guilt*, expressed psychically by *the superego function*. [1994, pp. 8–10]

The authors conclude that Fairbairn's description of the superego function provides a more plausible account of the results of deprivation and persecution in relationships than is the case with Freud's theory.

In his discussion, Fairbairn considers the question of whether the superego is "a composite of direct primary identifications" or, alternatively, "a congregate of lost objects". He also discusses whether Freud's superego was both an agent of repression and an object of repression, and concludes that the superego was not repressed, but was rather a "dissociated structure cut off from the main stream of mind" because it is incompatible with the ego. Here, then, was the seed of the later significance given to the role of splitting in mental life. His conclusion was that the superego was a functional aspect of the ego and not a separate structure (*ibid.*).

I turn next to a brief summary of Melanie Klein's theory of self, which, in contrast to Fairbairn, is an extension of the classical theory of the unconscious drives. According to Klein, a "sense of self" arises from a phantasy world dominated by internal objects, and which is omnipresent. The earliest phantasy system is built up in relation to part-objects (e.g., "the breast") and energized by primary aggressive drives. The infant experiences these part-objects as persecuting and dangerous, and, in response to them, it splits the representation of the mother into "good" and "bad" parts. This mental state is referred to as the paranoid–schizoid position (see Chapters Three and Four).

From Klein's standpoint, the infant psyche is constituted in a flux of phantasy, and is characterized by fragmentation, and suffused with primary paranoid and schizoid anxieties. These have their source in the "death instinct".

At this early stage, the primitive self is a rudimentary and precarious structure and, in the infant's imagination, it subjects the mother's body to violent attacks. This phantasized assault calls into use the primitive defences, i.e., splitting, projection, and projective identification. Although these are employed as an attempt at self-protection, in actuality they tend to empty and further weaken the ego–self. In the sequential pattern, the infant now comes to fear maternal retaliation and persecution, and the annihilation of the fragile self. In this situation, this self, in order to maintain its stability, integrity, and psychic survival, is reliant on taking in, by introjective identification, the more loving aspects of the caring object.

"Good" mental health is perceived as sustained when good experiences and affects dominate over bad ones and, in time, the weak and vulnerable ego–self becomes strengthened and integrated, and the perceived threat from the object is lessened.

If this early developmental situation is worked through successfully, the infant will gradually progress in the second six months of life towards the depressive position (see Chapters Three and Four). This is a state of mind that marks a developmental shift, i.e., an emotional change from relating to objects on a "part" basis to relating to them as whole persons. This achievement involves the infant's construction and perception of the mother as a unified, independent person who relates to others and who is seen as being both "good" and "bad". Such development is crucial to the establishment of selfhood, since the infant also comes to experience that he/she is also "the one, same self" that experiences both "good" and "bad" feelings. In health, this development enables the infant to experience and sustain primitive feelings of depressive anxiety, guilt, sorrow, and responsibility for its fantasized and real actions towards the other. This is the beginning of a basic concern about the other's fate, and the discovery of the possibility of reparation for the earlier (fantasized) damage to the object.

However, if, for either constitutional or environmental reasons, or both, the infant's hatred comes to predominate and the para-noid–schizoid state of mind remains in ascendancy, various pathologies of the self will result. When this situation prevails, the infant's object world continues to be constructed on the basis of fantasy rather than external reality, and the self-organization will remain at an immature, schizoid level. According to Klein, the external world becomes increasingly disconnected the more para-noid anxieties prevail over depressive anxieties. The emergence of a healthy, coherent, and autonomous self, then, is, for her, depen-dent on the successful negotiation of depressive affects and repara-tive drives, and on the possibility of experiencing a good internalized object (Klein, 1946).

Freud had understood projection as a channelling of uncon-scious drives towards objects, whereas Klein's theory gives more emphasis to an interactional process in which, in phantasy, the infant expels a part of the self and puts it into the other, i.e., "projec-tive identification". Her theory offers a very complex picture of mental dynamics between self and others, and gives greater emphasis to two-person psychology (Rickman, 1950; Stewart, 1996, p. 30).

However, in spite of its many strengths, a number of observers have pointed out that Klein's theory, with its focus on the internal phantasy world, tends to underplay the role of environment, soci-ety, and culture, in structuring personality and object relationships. In other words, since phantasy is seen as the primary source of self, what may become relatively neglected is the social context of phan-tasy formations, although, in fairness, this issue is perhaps ("a chicken or egg") paradoxical one that must remain unresolved.

Research in child development also suggests that early phan-tasies, as described by Klein, imply an awareness of spatial factors and a capacity to use symbols, which are not yet developed in the first year of life and cannot, therefore, be part of the developmental process at this time. It has also been observed that, in relation to

Freud's basic concept of drives, Klein's theories "imply a state of pre-natal suspended animation which does not ring true with personal experience or later research" (Gomez, 1997, p. 51. See also Holder, 2005).

I turn lastly to Donald Winnicott's account of how the infant comes to develop a sense of self. He considered his views to be an extension of Freud's work, and he also acknowledges a large debt to Klein. However, while he fully acknowledges the significance of the child's phantasy life (see, for example, his *Therapeutic Consultations in Child Psychiatry*, Winnicott, 1971), unlike Klein, he gives much greater emphasis to the early actual human environment.

For Winnicott, at the earliest stage, the infant is merged psychologically with the mother, and what he terms the ego–self's "unit status" is only later achieved when a coherent "ego" emerges from a weak and fragmented system of ego-nuclei. At that stage, the infant's state of mind is one of "unintegration" and, "in health", it will, only gradually, come to achieve a more integrated, personal ego–self. However, see Winnicott (1971) and Milner (1957), who stress the value of the capacity to regress to, and use, unintegrated states of mind in the service of creativity.

Elliott (1994) writes that Winnicott's selfhood

> depends on establishing the kind of relationship which is at once liberating and supportive, creative and dependent, defined and formless. For it is within this interplay of integration and separation that Winnicott locates the roots of authentic selfhood, creativity, and the process of symbolisation, as well as of social relations and culture. [p. 25]

In Winnicott's view, whether or not this happens in the individual case largely depends on the quantity and quality of "good-enough" mothering, which begins with the quality of the mother's state of "primary maternal preoccupation". It is the love and concern of the maternal object that gradually enables the infant to distinguish the "Me" from the "Not Me" and establish its own "unit status". This growth will, in time, lead to the formation of a core identity in the child ("a stable core of selfhood") and form a basis for an autonomous existence and a "going-on-being" in the social world (Winnicott, 1962, 1988).

His theory also places much emphasis on the distinction between a "true self" and a "false self". He associates the former with a sense of being real, a feeling of authenticity, the experience of aliveness, and, above all, with "creativity". The false self, on the other hand, is formed from an over-compliance with the mother's "demands, desires and feelings". Both selves are always present in varying degree in each individual, and the relationship between the two determines the normality and pathology of selfhood. In the extreme pathological state, a split-off, compliant false self leads to unconscious fragmentation, annihilation anxiety, and a sense of futility. These ideas are clearly linked to Fairbairn's schizoid state of being, and to Klein's paranoid–schizoid position.[3]

The critique of the Enlightenment, modernism, and psychoanalysis

Postmodern thought can be loosely described as a general scepticism about everything and everyone. Its overall approach questions the validity of the knowledge base of the Enlightenment, and of modernist thinkers. This critique is to be found in various theoretical writings under headings such as postmodernism, poststructuralism and deconstruction.[4]

The postmodern challenge is to the "Grand Theories", "stable essences", and cognitive and moral certainties of the Enlightenment and modernism that, it is argued, can no longer be trusted.[5]

The modernists had sought to establish a knowledge base which favoured "authority, universalisation, rationalisation, systemisation and consistent criteria for the evaluation of knowledge claims", whereas the postmodernists question the status of all knowledge associated with this approach (Taylor & Winquist, 2000, p. 304).

Psychoanalysis is considered by postmodernists to be an example of a search for a meta-narrative knowledge base, and is criticized on the grounds that it assumes that the exploration of the unconscious (via "reason" and "truth") will produce knowledge of the human situation that will be of universal relevance. In contrast, postmodern thought favours a preference for "little narratives" (defined as "cultural representations of local or minority subjects"), which have no privileged status or power, and thus cannot be applied in a more general sense (Lyotard, 1979; Macey, 2000).

A further criticism of psychoanalysis derives from the critique of the concept of "essentialism" (defined as "the permanent nature of being of a phenomenon").[6]

For example, the post-modernists reject the idea of essential, fixed gender categories and question the concept of an unchanging or eternal "female nature". What is particularly attacked is the idea of an "essentialist identity" that is implied in Freud's famous statement "Biology is destiny". This is considered invalid, because it is argued that it places the "feminine" outside the "process of self-constitution" (i.e., the theory that the formation of the subject is independent of a fixed gender category). The concept "Woman" is considered to be a structure observed in a socio-historical context. For example, Julia Kristeva (a Lacanian-inspired psychoanalyst) has stated that "Woman as such does not exist. She is in the process of becoming" (Kristeva, 1980, 1986).[7]

The whole idea of "identity" and "self", if regarded as "essences" (and, therefore, something "fixed" and immutable), has been much criticized by postmodern thinkers. These critics question the assumption of an "integrated, coherent solid state self" that can achieve individual autonomy and is capable of personal moral responsibility. They consider that this is an illusion (in the sense of a "fiction"). The postmodernists favour the view that, as modern science continuously re-establishes the boundaries of knowledge, assumptions such as universal normality, and equality, in moral responsibility need to be challenged.

It is noteworthy that the three object-relations theories described earlier have in common the idea of a "unified, integral ego" as a basis for development. From a postmodern standpoint, such an idea of self-development is questioned, since it involves the unfolding of a human essence (Elliott, 1994, p. 24).

A number of postmodern thinkers have also criticized the psychoanalytic enterprise on other grounds. For example, it is claimed that psychoanalysis is a system of knowledge that has arisen as a "product of sociohistorical and ideological forces". Their viewpoint emphasizes the relativity of knowledge in different cultures, and they question any tradition that relies on human reason and, therefore, the conceptual status of such Freudian concepts as the ego, the self, and the superego.

One of these critics, Foucault, has described how hidden "super-ego systems" function in modern society. Consistent with Freud's views, he regards the superego as part and parcel of ourselves, our ideals, and our self-judgements. However, in his view, it is also an actual reflection of identity itself. His major thesis suggests that a "Big Brother" not only functions outside of us (as in George Orwell's novel, *1984*), but inside us, directing our lives. This is the superego in its form of self-discipline, self-control, self-punishment, etc.

Foucault's critique of psychoanalysis is part of his questioning of the formation, and limitations, of all systems of thought. This leads him to challenge Freudian assumptions about the nature of sexuality and the concept of mental health. He examines such fundamental problems as how "Man" has come to know himself, and he seeks to demonstrate how the sciences of the past were formulated as modes of thought that were associated with a given historical period. He suggests that "madness", for example, is socially constructed by a wide variety of discourses, and he describes how these give rise to a collective definition of insanity. In summary, Foucault's work attempts to demonstrate how an Enlightenment value system such as Freud's (that stresses such values as personal autonomy, individualism, and moral responsi-bility) is actually underpinned by a power matrix (network of forces) that shapes these values (Foucault, 1969, 1975, 1976, 1984a,b).

A problem that arises in superego theory, and that has attracted both psychoanalytic and postmodern comment, is that of the conceptual status of "agency". Matte Blanco, for example, puts this issue as follows:

> I do not feel that my id tells my ego to do something and that my superego tells me not to do it. I feel instead, that I feel the desire to do it and that I feel I should not do it . . . the superego might be con-sidered exercising . . . super ego functions . . . in contrast to the cor-responding functions exercised by the central or main aspects of the self . . . we would have to conceive the mind, or a person, as a self, or a person with . . . different functions that can never exist indepen-dently from the self. [Matte Blanco, cited by Rayner, 1995, p. 115]

In this quotation, the overall dominance of the self is emphasized in relation to the superego. (Note that the "I" is repeated five times!)

Agency has been defined as "the state or capability to determine oneself and one's actions in an individual, collective, or otherwise social sense . . . the state of being present, active or self-actualised in the performance of political, ideological, philosophical selfhood" (Taylor & Winquist, 2000, p. 6).

The problem and complexity of defining personal agency, as distinct from the "internalized other" (i.e., "Whose voice is it?") is illustrated in the following quotation, in which the author describes the internalization process: "the means by which the imagined presence of another may (for better or worse) continue to control one's actions and intentions" (Church, 1991, p. 219).

The postmodern critic, Louis Althusser (1993), has questioned the extent of the idea of the subject's freedom and power to act or choose voluntarily and deliberately. He argues that, since all individuals are under the influence of specific ideologies, the subject's will or control to make decisions is limited, and the extent of this limitation varies with particular situations and circumstances.[8]

Discussion of the post-modern critique

It can be argued that Freud's great discoveries and his general research approach have, in some respects, a postmodern flavour. This is to be found, for example, in his continuous revision of concepts and models, his willingness to use art, mythology, and literature as supplements to empirical inquiry, and in his exploration of dreams, symptoms, and parapraxes. In other words, he sought to advance knowledge using multiple methods of data-gathering and levels of meaning. It can also be said that the results of this research are a demonstration that the idea of a conscious, unified mind (and the assumption that it controls thinking and feeling) has to be "deconstructed" and "decentralized", as emphasized by postmodernists.

From another angle, but one consistent with the viewpoint of the postmodernists, Freud's major thesis is an illustration of the non-unity of the human mind; i.e., the fundamental splits between consciousness, the preconscious, and the dynamic unconscious.

Among psychoanalysts, and many others, "the ego–self" is assumed to be a complex idea that combines both unity and diversity. It is assumed, for example, that the self, as experienced in one's own consciousness, and in its presentation to others, has a certain multiplicity and fluidity. However, this changeability does not amount to non-unity in the sense of the complete absence of coherence. I am suggesting, therefore, that, at least "in health", there always exists *a core self* which remains "grounded", in spite of the great variety of its manifestations. In this connection, Robert Lifton comments as follows:

> The protean self seeks to be both fluid and grounded, however tenuous that combination. There is nothing automatic about the enterprise, no "greening of the self", but rather a continuous effort without clear termination. Proteanism, then, is a balancing act between responsive shape shifting . . . and efforts to consolidate and cohere. [Lifton, 1993, p. 9]

Zygmunt Bauman, an eminent sociologist, has commented on the dominant negativity of much postmodern thinking, and points out how it "obscures our ability to analyse". He is especially critical of those intellectuals who lay claim to the ability and duty to act as the "collective conscience of the nation". However, his view of the "postmodern condition" is, nevertheless, that "it provides great challenges and great opportunities to the astute citizen". He suggests that, although concepts such as an *ideal autonomous agent* and *ethical objectivity* may be problematic, such moral language and ethical principles should, nevertheless, be maintained, and he advocates a model of inquiry that promotes "face to face encounters, the notion of ambiguity, the *concepts of psychoanalysis*, the practice of writing, and the primacy of the subject's self-formation" (Bauman, (1993). See also Kristeva (1980, 1986), Levinas (1972, 1974), Macey (2000, p. 34), Taylor and Winquist (2000, p. 252).

The issues that relate to the status of gender, and to superego theory, are many and complex. Significant criticisms have already been discussed in relation to Freud's views of superego development in females (Chapters Two and Three). However, it seems likely that there exist important psychobiological differences between women and men, and that these differences are then organized and refined by cultural factors. For example, in so far as the social expectations on women are greater than those on men, they are allowed less freedom than men for "self" experimentation.

These demands often involve women in a great deal of "'protean juggling', in which attempts are made to honour their commitments to home, childbirth, and nurturing, with their chosen occupational and intellectual pursuits" (Lifton, 1993).

The postmodern critique of the concept of a stable and coherent self fails to acknowledge a central paradox that exists in the "idea of a self" (or, more strictly speaking, "a sense of self"). I suggest that, "in health" at least, two main selves can be detected in the human situation. The first is the self that undergoes constant modification in line with continuous changes in our consciousness, and the second is a "core" self that has a relatively stable and continuous existence. That is, although there are clear limits to the idea of a core self, its theoretical acceptance has some important advantages.

The abandonment of a modernist viewpoint results in the birth of "the postmodern subject", and certain problems in this development have by no means escaped notice. I shall briefly discuss the work of two critics of postmodern ideas, Slavoj Žižek and George Frankl, who have written interesting and disturbing accounts of the postmodern approach.

The Lacanian philosopher, Slavoj Žižek, has produced a number of publications critical of the nature of what he refers to as the "post-modern superego". He perceives the superego in the New Age as: "a structure of power that demands a transgression of the (symbolic) Law, its suspension, and the identification with perverse enjoyment or jouissance" (Žižek, 1989).

According to Žižek, the development of this "new law" has been generated by the growth of the postmodern superego, and this results in what he refers to as "the universalised reflexivity of our lives". He means, by this phrase, the coming into being of a cultural process in which the individual person can experience his impulses as matters of choice, and in which he/she appears to be free to choose their own rules. He questions the aim of such "reflexivity" as being to "recover the spontaneity of our true selves". He suggests that the problem is that underlying the new law is, in fact, a reliance on a superego imperative of the kind: "Self-realisation is your duty". He suggests, further, that psychoanalysis has become one of the victims of this phenomenon of "reflexivization" (Wright, 1999; Wright & Wright, 1999; Žižek, 1992).

Žižek describes how the growth of this postmodern superego has accompanied the loss of parental authority and traditional values, thus influencing subject and object. In this new culture, he notes, and laments, the loss of the "symbolic order" and "code of accepted fictions", which formerly acted as guides in social behaviour.

He describes *a maternal superego* that forbids "normal enjoyment", and an *anal–sadistic father* who is "too alive", knows "too much" and commands "his own enjoyment", and considers this development to be to the detriment of the subject, who becomes denuded of resources.

Žižek also describes the goal of the postmodern subject as "pathologically narcissistic", in that it has become one of profound self-realization and "reshifting and reshaping multiple identities". In his view, the subject's conformity with this process results in more and more pressure coming from an ever-more punitive superego. The paradox (i.e., the "Catch 22")[9] in this new culture is that, "in the name of freedom", the subject's actual freedom of choice has, in fact, been undermined. According to Žižek, the essential content of the postmodern superego is *"Enjoy!"* (This command is of the order *"Now you had better enjoy it!"*)

To clarify this phenomenon, he offers the following illustration, which he compares with the traditional mode of symbolic paternal authority. In this example, the Kantian (repressive) mode of authority that gives rise to the parental command, "You must go to see your grandmother whether you want to or not", is contrasted with the postmodern superego command, "You should go only if you really want to. If you don't want to then stay at home".

However, he interprets this latter command in the following way. Suppose, he says, the child chooses to stay at home; this will produce the parental response, "How can you be so cruel . . . what did your poor grandmother do to make you not want to see her?"

He concludes that the postmodern superego is, therefore, deceptive, and only *appears* to offer a free choice when there really is no choice. In this instance, the child is actually being given an order and told "to smile at the same time". The postmodern superego's command to "Enjoy!" is an inversion of the Kantian imperative, in that the statement, "You can because you must", has now become "You must because you can" (Žižek , 1999).

The second critic of the postmodern condition, to whom I now turn, is George Frankl, who has also written extensively on the nature and problems of the "post-modern superego" (Frankl, 2000).

He points to a growing awareness that, at the beginning of the new millennium, humankind faces a "crisis of morality". In his view, this has developed as a result of the experience of "the killing fields", and other horrors of the major and minor wars, and of the numerous genocides and other failures (e.g., Third World poverty) of the so-called "enlightened" twentieth century.[10]

This human predicament comes about because of a failure of ethics, in that, in the current era, there is no definite and reliable knowledge of what is "good" and "bad", and "right" and "wrong", but what we have is a "fog" of uncertainty, and a "helpless confusion", and dread of the future.

Frankl considers the postmodern critique of the intellectual framework of the Enlightenment as an attack on the "collective superego" (he describes this as the "father figure which promised so much and failed so miserably"). However, like Žižek, he sees serious problems in the postmodern trend that has displaced the traditional superego, its constraints, and its maintenance of civilized values. He points to the dangers and disadvantages of the postmodern tendency to "defy dismiss and even annihilate" these moral constraints, while, at the same time, promoting the ego-self to align itself with the primitive drives of the id (i.e., in this respect, Freud's maxim for psychoanalytic treatment, "Where id was ego shall be", has been reversed to "Where ego was id shall be"). In his view, the danger of such a reversal is that it encourages the growth of a kind of "ego mania", which is advocated by "practitioners of the id" (e.g., in the slogan, "Greed is good!").

Frankl describes the "return of the repressed" and the liberation of greed, selfishness, and sadism, as "the new morality". He sees this cultural shift as a kind of inversion, in which aggression is directed towards what he calls "the own superego, the own culture". In this development, what has acquired a dominant role in the individual (and the group) is a "primitive narcissistic ego", and what Abraham originally described as an "oral cannibalistic drive".

In the concluding section of this chapter, and of the book, I consider my account of the system superego in relation to philosophical ideas of morality and ethics.

The superego, and the nature and growth of morality

The superego system of the individual is closely associated with the predominant morality of the society in which the person lives. The development of the system evolves through an internalization process, beginning with the parents, and continuing through a number of different influences that have been elaborated and discussed in Chapter Three. Gradually, as the system develops in the individual, it becomes increasingly associated with an abstract representation of a particular society's norms and ideals; that is, with a particular system of morality.

The British analyst, Pearl King, has recently edited and published the *Collected Papers of John Rickman*. These papers include an article that discusses the development of the superego and morality, and Rickman's commentary provides a useful addition to my own exploration and conclusions (King, 2003, pp. 314–335).

Rickman writes of the importance of the educator's significant role in interpreting the adult world to the child, and the "culture of the child to the adult world". In noting the human capacity for flexibility and adaptability in behavioural patterns, he emphasizes the significance of understanding how the moral function (particularly its "unconscious dimension", e.g., the process of defence) originates, and influences the development of the individual person.

His account describes the moral function as a "combination of a biological and a social function" (i.e., with roots partly in the individual's animal nature, and partly in the person's cultural inheritance). He stresses how the infant's "greatest need is for a stabiliser", and how one component of this is the moral, "protective" function (this protection, initially of "the self", later comes to protect the community). He describes two approaches to how the growth of the moral function can be understood. The first is via an idea of an external source (i.e., God as creator and model of an "ideal"), and the second through an investigation of how the individual adapts his biological endowment to the satisfaction of his/her cultural environment, in a series of slow and gradual stages, and in which things, at any stage, can go slightly or seriously wrong.

In describing the development of the superego, he says it is "an active process within the mind [which] meets a biological need . . . the total personality is involved in it, but it is an unconscious process", and he draws attention to its "liveliness" or "livingness" (i.e., something of an alive human quality *present* within us) as an important aspect of its functioning in the personality.

Rickman writes

> The inner world is a theatre ... in which the child ... [and adult] is forever playing over and over the emotional problems which preoccupy him ... the relation of the parents to one another ... [including fantasies of] having children, killing children and cooking and eating them, and reviving them again, and so on. [p. 324]

In a section on the source of moral feelings, he makes an important connection between aggression and the primitive sense of guilt, or what he calls "proto-guilt". "We feel guilt when and only when, we do or intend an injury to a loved object (person or thing or abstraction such as 'Truth')" (*ibid.*, p. 325). Rickman points to the presence of aggression and love within us from an early age that leads to guilt feelings ("pricks of conscience").

He also considers the "optimum development of the moral function", which he equates with the superego, and he stresses its functions (e.g., vigilance and protection) in relation to the "standards" of both society, and of the individual's ego ideal. Thus, for Rickman, the idea of a mature morality involves the protection of "self", as well as the "object". He also argues against any association with "mortification of the flesh and penances of the spirit", but favours a function that is "wholesome", life-giving and supportive. He says, further, that maturity of this kind cannot be implanted, but "only grows in its own time and in its own way" (*ibid.*, p. 328), and that it should also not be understood in a purely mechanical way, as, for example, "conformity to a standard of conduct". This would omit the necessity for such maturity to have a "personal" dimension, both in the thought process and in governing behaviour. He summarizes superego maturity of this kind in the following way:

> a sensitive perception of the codes of ethics in the community, but the person must not lose himself in an identification with that community [since] one of the values of morality is its highly individual quality ... one of its chief biological survival values. [*ibid.*, p. 328]

In the last sections of the paper, Rickman considers the question of cultural transmission, and emphasizes that superego maturity implies "ego–self" maturity, i.e., a personalized, independent approach to morality ("facing our own troubles as best we may"), rather than, say, a blind obedience to codes of conduct or parental admonitions, and he contrasts two kinds of cultural transmission. The first involves an *unabsorbed superego,* which is the more defensive, "noisy . . . reforming [and] intrusive". The second is a more *assimilated superego,* "personal, quieter and perhaps more wise" (*ibid.,* p. 333).

Finally, he offers a statement of the significant psychoanalytic dimension in the achievement of mature morality, in the following terms, which I quote selectively:

> Morality does not . . . consist in *doing* particular things and not doing others, but in . . . *feeling* the impulses of the love and hate, . . . first in [the self] . . . then in others, and choosing . . . the more constructive, the less disruptive, pathway in social relationships. The growth of the moral function [is] the change from dogmatism to exploration and choice; from sudden, all or none explosive responses in situations involving moral choice to graduated controlled responses; from reflex or reactive action to consideration; from automatism to love. (p. 333, author's italics).

Lastly in this section, I offer a final comment on the relationship between the superego and "morality". Although the superego can be understood to be the "agent" of morality in the way described by Freud and Rickman, it should be understood that the two concepts are closely connected but not logically equivalent (see Chapter One). The close association can be best seen when the superego issues commands that act against our self-interest (i.e., the *ought* aspect of living). However, the difference becomes clear when we note that some theories of morality do *not* have, as their requirement, behaviour that opposes self-interest, nor do they necessarily advocate moral acts that the subject feels obliged to carry out. Some moral philosophers have also suggested that the "moral conscience" and the superego should not be equated, because of a confusion of terminology. They point out, for example, that Freud commits a "category error" in using moral terminology (conscience, guilt feelings, remorse) ambiguously to describe and explain non-moral (i.e., psychological) phenomena (superego, repression, anxiety, and need for punishment) (see Deigh, 1984; Flugel, 1945; Jones, 1966).

Conclusion

This book commenced from the assumption that there is considerable value and relevance for the human situation, at the beginning of the new millennium, in Freud's tripartite division of the mind into ego, superego, and id. I have been concerned throughout to explore his contention that mental health can be associated with maintaining a balance and a harmony between these unconscious structures, such that the ego, so to speak, is "master in its own house". It follows that mental ill-health (psychopathology in its broadest sense) can be related to an imbalance in the mind, in which either the id or the superego has gained control, and is able to dominate to an extent detrimental to the subject, the object, and society.

I have referred to the superego as a "system" in which a number of elements (e.g., ego ideal, ego self, conscience, guilt, etc.) overlap and interact in a complex way. I have attempted, nevertheless, to describe, and to some extent distinguish, these features of the system, and to show how they come to have a profound effect on the personality and, therefore, on human relationships. In spite of my efforts, however, it remains true that the elements have resisted narrow definition, and have refused to be pinned down in a logical way.

What I hope has been more successful, in my exploration, is how the system, beginning in early infancy, develops gradually over time, so that, "in health", a maturity is achieved. However, I have emphasized that such an achievement, though relatively stable and reliable, can nevertheless be upset, so that, at any stage, the developmental process can become disturbed, and the individual's growth become subject to fixation and malign regression.

I have described how the development of the system depends on the quality of the interaction between the "subject" and the "object" in the widest sense (mother, father, carer, sibling, teacher, friend, authority figure, etc.). This development becomes firmly established when an "internalized other" becomes part of the mind and continues to mature as an aspect of the personal "self". Yet, the achievement of a mature superego also contains a hidden paradox, in that, although it is reliant on the internalization of the "other", it is only recognizable in the form of a relatively autonomous "free" self, i.e., one capable of making its own ethical decisions.

I have demonstrated various ways in which the superego system and its parts can malfunction to an extent that causes unbalance in the mind, and I have described how this may result in serious problems for the individual, and for society as a whole. I have suggested a twofold effect of such malfunctioning. In the first, "superego aggression" attacks and weakens the ego–self, which results in various types of psychopathology in the subject. In the second, the system itself may, under certain conditions, become weak or corrupted, so that the normal constraints on aggressive id impulses become inoperative, and these gain control of the personality and attack and/or destroy the "object".

Lastly, I have examined the relevance of the superego concept as a way of understanding, and gaining insight into, some of the problems and dilemmas faced by the human individual at the beginning of the new millennium. I suggest that certain dangers arise: first, when superego constraints are absent to an extent that favours the development of "ego mania", and second, when the culture of the "postmodern superego" issues commands in the hidden form of *"You Ought to!"*), which can be understood as a disguised, distorted and dangerous form of social control.

I end with a cliché, which may nevertheless be an apt summary of my point of view: The superego is a good servant but a bad master!

Notes

1. A statement from a fictional character, Robyn Penrose, in a novel.
2. Fairbairn considered what Freud saw as the superego to include this duo (the anti-libidinal ego/rejecting object), together with the aspirations and expectations supplied by the ideal object in relation to the central ego.
3. For a critique of Winnicott's work, see Greenberg and Mitchell (1983) and Gomez (1997).
4. Postmodernism and poststructuralism are not easy to define or describe, because they are not unitary or single philosophical move-

ments. In the literature, the notion of a *postmodern perspective* is used for those critics who seek to examine the sources and assumptions behind "institutionalized knowledge", and to expose the nature of "power relations", and the contingent nature of authority, gender, identity, etc. In postmodern writings, there is a repetition of, and emphasis on, certain concepts, e.g., *fragmentation, dislocation, contingency, uncertainty, flux, turbulence and risk* (Appignanesi & Garratt, 1999).

5. See Frankl (2000, p. 7).

6. The concept of "essentialism" probably derives from the Aristotelian distinction between "essence" and "accidents", in relation to the nature of things.

7. The Lacanian viewpoint is critical of Freud's essentialist standpoint, and of the assumption of a rational historical process that assumes linear, purposeful time.

8. Althusser has sought to make a conceptual link between Marxism and psychoanalysis, in his theory of ideology as "interpellation". In a comment on the status of "agency", he suggests that individuals are the "supports" and not the "agents" of historical processes, which are impersonal. He also writes that history is not a single process, but a complex combination of trends that develop in accordance with different rhythms.

9. *Catch 22* is the title of a novel by Joseph Heller, published in 1961. The title became famous as a description of a person who is put in a double-bind situation in which there is no way out.

10. For a commentary on this problem, which makes an interesting use of the superego concept, see Montgomery-Byles (2003).

REFERENCES

Abram, J. (1996). *The Language of Winnicott: A Dictionary of Winnicott's Use of Words*. London: Karnac.

Althusser, L. (1993). *Ecrits sur la psychanalyse*. Paris: Stock/IMEC.

Appignanesi, R., & Garratt, C. (1999). *Introducing Postmodernism*. New York: Icon.

Balint, M. (1954). Analytic training and training analysis. In: *Primary Love and Psychoanalytic Technique* (2nd edn, revised) (pp. 275–285). London: Tavistock, 1965.

Balint, M. (1968). *The Basic Fault: Therapeutic Aspects of Regression*. London: Tavistock.

Barnett, B. R. (2001). A comparison of the thought and work of Donald Winnicott and Michael Balint. In: M. Bertolini, A. Giannakoulas, & M. Hernandez (Eds.), *Squiggles and Spaces: Revisiting the Work of D. W. Winnicott* (pp. 189–195). London: Whurr.

Barnett, B. R. (2006). The capacity for concern, the novel *Catch 22* and modern war: a discussion. Public Lecture given at the Centre for Psychotherapy, Knockbracken Health Park, Belfast, Northern Ireland.

Bauman, Z. (1993). *Postmodern Ethics*. Oxford: Blackwell.

Bergmann, M. (1982). Thoughts on superego pathology of survivors and their children. In: M. S. Bergman & M. E. Yucovi (Eds.), *Generations of The Holocaust* (pp. 287–309). New York: Basic Books.

Bergmann, M. S., & Yucovi, M.E. (Eds.) (1982). *Generations of The Holocaust.* New York: Basic Books.

Berkowitz, R. (1999). The potential for trauma in the transference and countertransference. In: S. Johnson & S. Ruszczynsky (Eds.), *Psychoanalytic Psychotherapy in the Independent Tradition* (pp. 111–132). London: Karnac.

Bernstein, D. (1983). The female superego: a different perspective. *International Journal of Psychoanalysis, 64*: 187–201.

Bion, W. R. (1957). Differentiation of the psychotic from the nonpsychotic personality. In: *Second Thoughts* (pp. 43–64). London: Maresfield Library, 1967.

Bion, W. R. (1959). Attacks on linking. In: *Second Thoughts* (pp. 93–109). London: Maresfield Library, 1967.

Bion, W. R. (1962). *Learning From Experience.* London: William Heineman Medical.

Bion, W. R. (1967). *Second Thoughts.* London: Maresfield Library.

Bion, W. R. (2000). *Clinical Seminars and Other Works.* London: Karnac.

Blamires, A. (1984). *A Portrait of The Artist As A Young Man* (York Notes, Longman Literature Guide). Harlow: Longman York.

Blos, P. (1967). The second individuation process of adolescence. *Psychoanalytic Study of the Child, 22*: 162–186.

Blos, P. (1972). The function of the ego ideal in adolescence. *Psychoanalytic Study of the Child, 29*: 43–88.

Blum, H. P. (1976). Masochism, the ego ideal, and the psychology of women. *Journal of American Psychoanalytic Association, 24*(Suppl.): 157–191.

Bott-Spillius, E. (1988). *Melanie Klein Today: Developments in Theory and Practice.* Vol. 1, 'Mainly Theory'. London and New York: Tavistock and Routledge.

Britton, R. (2003). *Sex, Death, and the Superego: Experiences in Psychoanalysis.* London: Karnac.

Brookner, A. (1988). *Latecomers.* London: Jonathon Cape.

Brown, L. (1993). *The New Shorter Oxford English Dictionary: On Historical Principles.* Oxford: Clarendon Press.

Browning, C. R. (1992). *Ordinary Men: Reserve Police Battalion 101 and the Final Solution in Poland.* New York: Harper-Perennial

Buckley, P. (1986). *Essential Papers on Object Relations*. New York: New York University Press.

Chasseguet-Smirgel, J. (1970). *Female Sexuality: New Psychoanalytic Views*. Ann Arbor, MI: University of Michigan Press.

Chasseguet-Smirgel, J. (1975). *The Ego Ideal: A Psychoanalytical Essay on the Malady of the Ideal*. London: Free Association, 1984.

Church, J. (1991). Morality and the internalised other. In: J. Neu (Ed.), *The Cambridge Companion to Freud* (pp. 209–223). Cambridge: Cambridge University Press.

Cohen, E. A. (1988). *Human Behaviour in the Concentration Camp*. London: Free Association.

Coltart, N. (1992). *Slouching Towards Bethlehem . . . and Further Psychoanalytic Explorations*. London: Free Association.

Davis, M., & Wallbridge, D. (1981). *Boundary and Space: An Introduction to the Work of D. W. Winnicott*. London: Karnac.

Deigh, J. (1984). Remarks on some difficulties in Freud's theory of moral development. *International Review of Psychoanalysis*, 11(2): 207–225.

Edgcumbe, R. (2000). *Anna Freud, Frameworks: A View of Development, Disturbance and Therapeutic Techniques*. London: Routledge.

Ekins, R., & Freeman, R. (Eds.) (1994). *Centres and Peripheries of Psychoanalysis: An Introduction to Psychoanalytic Studies*. London: Karnac.

Eliot, G. (1876). *Daniel Deronda*. London: Everyman, 2000.

Elliott, A. (1994). *Psychoanalytic Theory: An Introduction*. Oxford: Blackwell.

Etchegoyen, R. H. (1991). *The Fundamentals of Psychoanalytic Technique*. London: Karnac.

Fairbairn, W. R. (1931). Features in the analysis of a patient with a physical genital abnormality. *Psychoanalytic Studies of the Personality* (pp. 197–222). London: Tavistock/Routledge & Kegan Paul, 1952.

Fairbairn, W. R. (1943). The repression and the return of bad object (with special reference to the 'war neuroses'). *Psychoanalytic Studies of the Personality* (pp. 59–81). London: Tavistock/Routledge & Kegan Paul.

Fairbairn, W. R. (1944). Endopsychic structure considered in terms of object-relationships. *Psychoanalytic Studies of the Personality* (pp. 82–136). London: Tavistock/Routledge & Kegan Paul.

Fairbairn, W. R. (1946). Object relations and dynamic structure. *Psychoanalytic Studies of the Personality* (pp. 137–151). London: Tavistock/Routledge & Kegan Paul.

Fairbairn, W. R. (1949). Steps in the development of an object-relations theory of the personality. *Psychoanalytic Studies of the Personality* (pp. 152–161). London: Tavistock/Routledge & Kegan Paul, 1952.

Fairbairn, W. R. (1952). *Psychoanalytic Studies of the Personality.* London: Tavistock/Routledge & Kegan Paul.

Fairbairn, W. R. (1958). On the nature and aims of psycho-analytical treatment. *International Journal of Psychoanalysis, 29*(5): 374–385.

Fairbairn, W. R. (1963). Synopsis of an object relations theory of the personality. *International Journal of Psychoanalysis, 44*: 224–225.

Fairbairn-Birtles, E., & Scharff, D. E. (Eds.) (1994). *From Instinct To Self: Selected Papers of W. R. D. Fairbairn.* Vol. 2. Northvale, NJ: Jason Aronson.

Fenichel, O. (1945). *The Psychoanalytic Theory of Neurosis.* New York: Psychoanalytic Quarterly.

Ferenczi, S. (1924). *Further Contributions to the Theory and Technique of Psychoanalysis.* New York: Basic Books, 1952.

Flugel, J. C. (1945). *Man, Morals and Society: A Psycho-analytic Study.* New York: International Universities Press.

Foucault, M. (1969). *The Archaeology of Knowledge.* A. M. Sheridan-Smith (Trans.). London: Tavistock, 1972.

Foucault, M. (1975). *Discipline and Punish: The Birth of the Prison.* A. M. Sheridan-Smith (Trans.). London: Allan Lane, 1977.

Foucault, M. (1976). *The History Of Sexuality (Vol.1): An Introduction* (R. Hurley, Trans.). London: Allan Lane, 1979.

Foucault, M. (1984a). The use of pleasure. In: *The History Of Sexuality (Vol. 2).* (R. Hurley, Trans.). Harmondsworth: Penguin, 1987.

Foucault, M. (1984b). The care of the self. In: *The History of Sexuality (Vol. 3).* R. Hurley (Trans.). Harmondsworth: Penguin, 1987.

Frankl, G. (2000). *Foundations of Morality: An Investigation into the Origin and Purpose of Moral Concepts.* London: Open Gate Press.

Freeman, T. (1998). *But Facts Exist: An Enquiry into Psychoanalytic Theorizing.* London: Karnac.

Freud, A. (1927a). Four lectures on child analysis. In: *Introduction to Psychoanalysis* (pp. 3–69). London: Hogarth, 1974.

Freud, A. (1927b). *The Psycho-Analytic Treatment of Children.* London: Imago, 1946.

Freud, A. (1936). *The Ego and the Mechanisms of Defence.* London: Hogarth.

Freud A. (1958). Adolescence. *Psychoanalytic Study of the Child, 3:* 225–278.

Freud, A. (1968). Panel Discussion with J. Arlow (Mod), J. Lampl-de Groot, & D. Beres. *International Journal of Psychoanalysis, 49*: 506–512.

Freud, S. (1895d). Psychotherapy of hysteria. In: *Studies on Hysteria, S.E., 2*: 269 and 282. London: Hogarth.

Freud, S. (1900a). Distortion in dreams. In: *The Interpretation of Dreams* (Part 1), *S.E., 4*: 142–143. London: Hogarth.

Freud, S. (1905e/1905d). Fragment of an analysis of a case of hysteria; *Three Essays on Sexuality. S.E., 7.* London: Hogarth.

Freud. S. (1912–1913). The return of totemism in childhood totem and taboo (Part 4). *S.E., 13: 141–142.* London: Hogarth.

Freud, S. (1914c). "On narcissism: an introduction". *S.E., 14*: 67–104. London: Hogarth.

Freud, S. (1917e). Mourning and melancholia. *S.E., 14*: 237–260. London: Hogarth.

Freud, S. (1921c). *Group Psychology and the Analysis of the Ego. S.E., 18*: 67–134. London: Hogarth.

Freud, S. (1923b). *The Ego and the Id. S.E., 19*, 3–63.

Freud, S. (1924c). *The Economic Problem of Masochism. S.E., 19*: 157–170. London: Hogarth.

Freud, S. (1925d). An autobiographical study. *S.E., 20*: 77–175. London: Hogarth.

Freud, S. (1926d). *Inhibitions, Symptoms and Anxiety. S.E.,* London: Hogarth.

Freud, S. (1927c). *The Future of an Illusion. S.E., 21*: 3–58 and 59–148.

Freud, S. (1930a). *Civilization and Its Discontents. S.E. 21*: 59–145. London: Hogarth.

Freud, S. (1933a). *New Introductory Lectures On Psycho-Analysis and Other Works. S.E., 22.* London: Hogarth.

Freud, S. (1933a). Femininity. *New Introductory Lectures On Psychoanalysis and Other Works. S.E., 22*: 112–135. London: Hogarth.

Freud, S. (1933a)[1932]. The dissection of the psychical personality. *New Introductory Lectures on Psychoanalysis and Other Works. S.E. 22: 57–80.*

Freud, S. (1936a). A disturbance of memory on the Acropolis. *S.E., 22*: 239–250. London: Hogarth.

Freud, S. (1940a[1938]). An outline of psychoanalysis. *S.E., 23*: 141–205. London: Hogarth.

Gilbert, G. M. (1950). Cited by Cohen (1988).

Glover, E. (1932). A psychoanalytic approach to the London Classification of Mental Disorders. In: *On The Early Development of Mind* (Chapter 11, pp. 161–186). London: Imago.

Gomez, L. (1997). *An Introduction to Object Relations*. London: Free Association.

Greenacre, P. (1952). *Trauma, Growth and Personality*. New York: Norton.

Greenberg, J. R., & Mitchell, S. R. (1983). *Object Relations in Psychoanalytic Theory*. Cambridge. MA: Harvard University Press.

Grinberg, L., Sor, D., & Tabak de Bianchedi, E. (1993). *New Introduction to the Work of Bion* (revised edn). Northdale, NJ: Jason Aronson.

Guntrip, H. (1961). *Personality Structure and Human Interaction: The Developing Synthesis of Psychodynamic Theory*. London: Hogarth.

Guntrip, H. (1968). *Psychoanalytical Theory, Therapy and the Self*. New York: Basic Books.

Guntrip, H. (1971). *Schizoid Phenomena, Object Relations and the Self*. London: Hogarth.

Gutt, A. (1935). *The Structure of Public Health in the Third Reich*. Cited by Cohen, E. 1988.

Handley, G. (1984). Introduction. In: *Daniel Deronda*. Oxford: Oxford University Press, The World's Classics Series.

Hayman, A. (1989). What do we mean by "phantasy"? *International Journal of Psychoanalysis*, 70: 105–114.

Hinshelwood, R. D. (1989). *A Dictionary of Kleinian Thought*. London: Free Association.

Holder, A. (1982). Preoedipal contributions to the formation of the superego. *Psychoanalytic Study of the Child*, 37: 245–272.

Holder, A. (2005). *Anna Freud, Melanie Klein, and the Psychoanalysis of Children and Adolescents*. London: Karnac.

Horne, A. (2006). Interesting things to say – and why. In: M. Lanyado and A. Horne (pp. 224–238). London: Routledge.

Horney, K. (1926). The flight from womanhood: the masculinity complex in women as viewed by men and women. *International Journal of Psychoanalysis*, 7: 324–339.

Hurry, A. (Ed.) (1998). *Psychoanalysis and Developmental Therapy*. London: Karnac.

Isaacs, S. (1948). On the nature and function of phantasy. *International Journal of Psychoanalysis*, 29, 73–97.

Johnson, S., & Ruszczynsky, S. (Eds.) (1999). *Psychoanalytic Psychotherapy in the Independent Tradition*. London: Karnac.

Jacobson, E. (1937). Ways of female superego formation and the female castration conflict. *Psychoanalytic Quarterly*, 45: 525–538.

Jacobson, E. (1964). *The Self and the Object World*. New York: International Universities Press.

Jones, D. H. (1966). Freud's theory of moral conscience. *Philosophy* 41: 155, 34–57.

Jones, E. (1927). The early development of female sexuality. In: *Papers On Psychoanalysis* (5th edn). London: Maresfield Reprints.

Joyce, J. (1992/1916). *Portrait of the Artist as a Young Man*. London: Penguin.

Karpf, A. (1996). *The War After: Living With The Holocaust*. London: Heinemann.

Kermode, F. (1997). *The Riverside Shakespeare* (2nd edn). H. Baker, A. Barton, F. Kermode, H. Levin, H. Smith, & M. Edel (Eds.). Boston: Houghton Mifflin.

Kestenberg, J. S. (1993). What a psychoanalyst learned from the Holocaust and Genocide. *International Journal of Psychoanalysis*, 74: 1117–1129.

Kestenberg, J. S., & Brenner, I. (1996). *The Last Witness: The Child Survivor of the Holocaust* (pp. 53–68). Washington, DC: American Psychiatric Press.

Kernberg, O. F. (1975). *Borderline Conditions and Pathological Narcissism*. Northvale, NJ: Jason Aronson.

King, P. (2003). *No Ordinary Psychoanalyst: The Exceptional Contributions of John Rickman*. London: Karnac.

King, P. & Steiner, R. (Eds.) (1991). *The Freud–Klein Controversies 1941–1945*. London: Tavistock/Routledge.

Klein, M. (1928). Early stages of the Oedipus conflict. In: *The Writings Of Melanie Klein. Vol.1* (pp. 186–198). London: Hogarth.

Klein, M. (1929). Infantile anxiety situations reflected in a work of art and in the creative impulse, in *The Writings Of Melanie Klein. Vol. 1* (pp. 210–218). London: Hogarth.

Klein, M. (1930). The importance of symbol formation in the development of the child in *The Writings of Melanie Klein* (pp. 219–232). London: Hogarth.

Klein, M. (1932). *The Psychoanalysis of Children*. London: Hogarth.

Klein, M. (1933). The early development of conscience in the child. In: *The Writings of Melanie Klein* (pp. 344–369). London: Hogarth.

Klein, M. (1934). On criminality. *British Journal of Medical Psychology*, 14: 312–315.

Klein, M. (1935). A contribution to the psychogenesis of manic–depressive states. *International Journal Psychoanalysis*, 16: 145–174.

Klein, M. (1940). Mourning and its relation to manic–depressive states. *International Journal of Psychoanalysis*, 21: 125–153.

Klein, M. (1946). Notes on some schizoid mechanisms. *International Journal of Psychoanalysis, 27*: 99–110.

Klein, M. (1948). *Contributions to Psycho-Analysis, 1921–45*. London: Hogarth.

Kogan, I. (1995). *The Cry of Mute Children: A Psychoanalytic Perspective of the Second Generation of the Holocaust*. London: Free Association.

Kohlberg, L. (1969). State and sequence. In: D. A. Gosling (Ed.), *Handbook of Socialization Theory and Research*. Chicago, IL: Rand McNally.

Krell, R., & Sherman, M. I. (1997). *Medical and Psychological Effects of Concentration Camps on Holocaust Survivors*. New Brunswick: Transaction.

Kristeva, J. (1980). Postmodernism? In: H. R. Garvin (Ed.), *Romanticism, Modernism, Postmodernism* (pp. 136–141). Lewisburg: Bucknell University Press.

Kristeva, J. (1986). *The Kristeva Reader*. T. Moi (Ed.) Oxford: Blackwell.

Lanyado, M., & Horne, A. (Eds.) (2006). *A Question of Technique: Independent Psychoanalytic Approaches with Children and Adolescents*. London: Routledge.

Laplanche, J., & Pontalis, J. B. (1973). *The Language of Psycho-Analysis*. London: Hogarth Press.

Levinas, E. (1972). *Humanisme de l'autre homme*. Montpellier: Fata Morgana.

Levinas, E. (1974). *Autrement qu'etre ou que dela de l'essence*. The Hague: Martinus Nijhoff.

Lewis, H. B. (1987). *Sex and the Superego: Psychic War in Men and Women* (revised edn). London: Lawrence Erlbaum.

Lifton, R. J. (1986). *The Nazi Doctors: Medical Killing and the Psychology of Genocide*. New York: Basic Books.

Lifton, R. J. (1993). *The Protean Self: Human Resilience in an Age of Fragmentation*. New York: Basic Books.

Lifton, R. J. and Markusen, E. (1988). *The Genocidal Mentality: Nazi Holocaust and Nuclear Threat*. London: MacMillan.

Lodge, D. (2002). *Consciousness and the Novel*. London: Secker and Warburg.

Lukacher, N. (1994). *Daemonic Figures: Shakespeare and the Question of Conscience*. Ithaca, NY: Cornell University Press.

Lyotard, J.-F. (1979). *The Postmodern Condition: A Report on Knowledge*. G. Bennington & B. Musumi (Trans.). Manchester: Manchester University Press, 1984.

Macey, D. (2000). *The Penguin Dictionary of Critical Theory*. London: Penguin.

Miller, J. B. (1988). *Toward A New Psychology of Women*. London: Penguin.

Milner, M. (1957). *On Not Being Able To Paint* (2nd edn). London: Heinemann, 1971.

Milrod, D. (1972). Self-pity, self-comforting and the superego. *Psychoanalytic Study of the Child, 27*: 505–528.

Modell, A. H. (1993). *The Private Self*. Cambridge, MA: Harvard University Press.

Mollon, P. (2003). *Shame and Jealousy: The Hidden Turmoils*. London: Karnac.

Montgomery-Byles, J. (2003). Psychoanalysis and war: the superego and projective identification. *Journal for the Psychoanalysis of Culture and Society, 8*, 2: 208–213.

Muller-Braunschweig, C. (1926). The genesis of the feminine superego. *International Journal of Psychoanalysis, 7*: 359–363.

Muslin, H. L. (1972). The superego in women. In: S. C. Post (Ed.), *Moral Values and The Superego Concept* (pp. 101–125). New York: International Universities Press.

Neu, J. (Ed.) (1991). *The Cambridge Companion to Freud*. Cambridge: Cambridge University Press.

Olsen, O. A., & Koppe, S. (1988). *Freud's Theory Of Psychoanalysis*. New York: New York University Press.

O'Shaughnessy, E. (1999). Relating to the superego. *International Journal of Psychoanalysis, 80*: 861–870.

O'Shaughnessy, E. (2005). Whose Bion? *International Journal of Psychoanalysis, 86*: 1523–1528.

Pines, D. (1993). *A Woman's Unconscious Use of Her Body*. London: Virago.

Rayner, E. (1978). *Human Development: An Introduction to the Psychodynamics of Growth, Maturity and Ageing* (2nd edn). London: George Allen & Unwin.

Rayner, E. (1995). *Unconscious Logic: An Introduction To Matte Blanco's Bi-Logic and its Uses*. London and New York: Routledge.

Reich, A. (1953). Narcissistic object choice in women. *Journal of the American Psychoanalytic Association, 1*: 22–44.

Rickman, J. (1950). The factor of number in individual and group dynamics. In: W. C. M. Scott (Ed.), *Selected Contributions To Psychoanalysis. J. Rickman*. London: Hogarth, 1957.

Rickman, J. (1951). The development of the moral function. In: P. King (Ed.), *No Ordinary Psychoanalyst: The Exceptional Contributions of John Rickman* (pp. 314–336). London: Karnac, 2003.

Riesenberg-Malcolm, R. (Ed.) (1999). *On Bearing Unbearable States of Mind.* London: Routledge.

Rosenberg, V. (1999). Erotic transference and its vicissitudes in the countertransference. In: S. Johnson & S. Ruszczynski (Eds.), *Psychoanalytic Psychotherapy in the Independent Tradition* (pp. 133–150). London: Karnac.

Rosenfeld, H. (1952). Notes on the psychoanalysis of the superego conflict of an acute schizophrenic patient. In: E. Bott-Spillius (Ed.), *Melanie Klein Today: Developments in Theory and Practice, Volume 1: Mainly Theory* (pp. 14–51). London: Tavistock and Routledge, 1988.

Roth, P. (2001). *The Superego.* Cambridge: Icon Books, Ideas in Psychoanalysis Series.

Rycroft, C. (1968). *A Critical Dictionary of Psychoanalysis.* London: Nelson.

Sachs, H. (1929). One motive factor in formation of superego in women. *International Journal of Psychoanalysis, 10:* 39–50.

Sandler, J. (1987). The concept of superego. In: *From Safety to Superego: Selected papers of Joseph Sandler.* London: Karnac.

Sandler, J., & Sandler, A.-M. (1998). *Internal Objects Revisited.* London: Karnac.

Schafer, R. (1960). The loving and beloved superego in Freud's structural theory. *Psychoanalytic Study of the Child, 15:* 163–188.

Schafer, R. (1974). Problems in Freud's psychology of women. *Journal of the American Psychoanalytic Association, 22:* 459–485.

Scharff, J. S. (Ed.) (1994). *The Autonomous Self: The Work of John D. Sutherland.* Northdale, NJ: Jason Aronson.

Segal, H. (1978). *Introduction to the Work of Melanie Klein.* London: Hogarth.

Sereny, G. (1995). *Albert Speer: His Battle With Truth.* London: Macmillan.

Settlage, C. (1993). Therapeutic process and developmental process in the reconstructing of object and self constancy. *Journal of the American Psychoanalytic Association, 41:* 473–492.

Sohn, L. (2000). The concept of the envious/jealous superego. In: J. Symington (Ed.) *Imprisoned Pain And Its Transformation: A Festschrift for H. Sydney Klein* (pp. 199–212). London: Karnac.

Steiner, R., & Johns, J. (Eds.) (2001). *Within Time and Beyond Time: A Festschrift for Pearl King*. London: Karnac.

Stewart, H. (1996). A theory of trauma and psychoanalytic education. *Michael Balin: Object Relations Pure and Applied* (pp. 61–67). London: Routledge.

Storr, A. (1968). *Human Aggression*. London: Allen Lane, Penguin.

Strachey, J. (1934). The nature of the therapeutic action of psychoanalysis. *International Journal of Psychoanalysis, 15*: 127–159.

Strachey, J. (1964). An outline of psychoanalysis, Editor's Note. In: *Moses and Monotheism, An Outline of Psychoanalysis and Other Works, S.E., 23* (1937/1939). London: Hogarth.

Taylor, V. E., & Winquist, C. E. (2001). *Encyclopaedia of Postmodernism*. London: Routledge.

Twain, M. (1884). *Adventures of Huckleberry Finn* (a Norton Critical Edition). New York: Norton.

Tyson, P., & Tyson, R. L. (1990). *Psychoanalytic Theories of Development: An Integration*. New Haven, CT: Yale University Press.

Waddell, M. (1998). *Inside Lives: Psychoanalysis and the Development of the Personality*. London: Duckworth.

Wardi, D. (1992). *Memorial Candles: Children of the Holocaust*. London: Routledge.

Wilson, S. (1984). Character development in *Daniel Deronda*: a psychoanalytic view. *International Review of Psychoanalysis, 11*: 199–206.

Winnicott, D. W. (1945). Primitive emotional development. In: *Collected Papers: Through Paediatrics to Psychoanalysis* (pp. 145–156). London: Tavistock, 1958,

Winnicott, D. W. (1958a). *Collected Papers: Through Paediatrics to Psychoanalysis*. London: Tavistock.

Winnicott, D. W. (1958b). Psychoanalysis and the sense of guilt. In: *The Maturational Processes and The Facilitating Environment: Studies in the Theory of Emotional Development* (pp. 15–28). London: Hogarth, 1979.

Winnicott, D. W. (1959–1964). Classification: is there a psychoanalytic contribution to psychiatric classification? In: *The Maturational Processes and The Facilitating Environment: Studies in the Theory of Emotional Development* (pp. 124–139). London: Hogarth, 1965.

Winnicott, D. W. (1960a). The theory of the parent–infant relationship. In: *The Maturational Processes and the Facilitating Environment: Studies in the Theory of Emotional Development* (pp. 37–55). London: Hogarth, 1965.

Winnicott, D. W. (1960b) Ego distortion in terms of true and false self. In: *The Maturational Processes and The Facilitating Environment: Studies in the Theory of Emotional Development,* 1965. 140–152.

Winnicott, D. W. (1962). Ego integration in child development. In: *The Maturational Processes and The Facilitating Environment: Studies in the Theory of Emotional Development* (pp. 56–63). London: Hogarth, 1965.

Winnicott, D. W. (1963). Morals and education. In: *The Maturational Processes and the Facilitating Environment: Studies in the Theory of Emotional Development* (pp. 100–105). London: Hogarth, 1965.

Winnicott, D. W. (1971a). *Playing and Reality.* London: Routledge.

Winnicott, D W. (1971b). The use of an object and relating through indentifications. In *Playing and Reality* (paperback, 1991) (pp. 86–94). London: Routledge.

Winnicott, D. W. (1971c). *Therapeutic Consultations in Child Psychiatry.* New York: Basic Books.

Winnicott, D. W. (1988). *Human Nature.* London: Free Association.

Wise, I. (Ed.) (2000). *Adolescence.* London: The Institute of Psychoanalysis.

Wright, E. (1999). *Speaking Desires Can Be Dangerous: The Poetics of the Unconscious.* Cambridge: Polity.

Wright, E., & Wright, E. (Eds.) (1999). *The Žižek Reader.* Oxford: Blackwell.

Zetzel, E. (1970). *The Capacity For Emotional Growth.* London: Maresfield Library.

Žižek, S. (1989). *The Sublime Object of Idealogy.* London: Verso

Žižek, S. (1992). *Enjoy Your Symptom!* New York: Routledge.

Žižek, S. (1999). You may! *London Review of Books,* 21(6), 18 March: 3–6.

INDEX